FOUR SURVIVOR GRANDPARENTS

RUN. RELY. REBUILD.

JONATHAN SCHLOSS

ISBN 9789493418462 (ebook)

ISBN 9789493418448 (paperback)

ISBN 9789493418455 (hardcover)

Publisher: Amsterdam Publishers, The Netherlands, 2025

info@amsterdampublishers.com

Four Survivor Parents is part of the series Holocaust Heritage

Copyright © Jonathan Schloss, 2025

Book Cover Design: Miriam Schloss

All Rights Reserved. No part of this publication may be reproduced or transmitted in any form or by any means, electronic or mechanical, including photocopy, recording or any other information storage and retrieval system, without prior permission in writing from the publisher.

CONTENTS

Introduction   ix

Piecing Together Acts I, II, and III   1
Four Survivor Grandparents   3

About the Author   195
Amsterdam Publishers Holocaust Library   197

"כתב זאת זכרון בספר"

"Write this as a remembrance in the Book..." (Exodus 17:14)

Dedicated to Nana & Papa, Grandma & Grandpa

and their parents and siblings:

Chaskel Dreksler & Bracha (née Naprzykszona) Dreksler

Irving Dreksler*

Shifra Dreksler

Toba Leah Dreksler

Nachum Wimmer & Serkei (née Palak) Wimmer

Elkan Hirsch ("Henyek") Wimmer

Solomon Wimmer

Sheva Wimmer

Menachem Mendel Kamelgarn* & Breindel Bronia (née Dzialoszynski) Kamelgarn

Murray Kamelgarn*

Leah Kamelgarn

Jacob Szlas & Miriam (née Mishler) Szlas

Isaac Szlas

Paja Szlas

Clara Szlas

and everyone else listed on a 4th grade homework assignment (below) whose lives and experiences inspired this book.

I am proud to have recorded your story and legacy.

*survived

Sam and Fay Schloss, August 1996

Sally and Jack Wimmer, August 1996

INTRODUCTION

Before the dark clouds of World War II engulfed Europe, four Jewish teenagers from different parts of Poland lived comfortable, normal lives until their families and communities were destroyed. It would have been easy to give up.

With his blond hair and blue eyes, Shaya Szlas assumed the identity of an orphaned Polish Catholic farmer to evade Nazi persecution. Urged by his mother's last plea to run to the forest and keep running, he hid in Eastern Poland's forests, barns, and farms, constantly staying a step ahead to avoid detection or capture, fearing he might be the last Jew on Earth. Feigele Kamelgarn rarely spoke about her time in the Lodz Ghetto or Auschwitz. She preferred to dish out unadulterated love and cling to family. Eventually, her family understood why.

Ripped from his family in a Kraków suburb, Joachim "Romek" Wimmer was forced into labor for the Nazi war machine at a munitions factory. Amid the horrors of random beatings and murders, he forged unbreakable bonds with fellow prisoners. They collectively defied despair by supporting one another. Decades later, as a business leader in the United States, he would give court testimony bringing a Nazi murderer to justice. Also separated from her family in Dąbrowa Górnicza, Sala Dreksler was forced to sew Nazi uniforms. She and other young women learned how to expertly handle threads and needles as if their lives depended on it – because it did.

Throughout World War II, Shaya and Feigele, Romek and Sala regularly had to make split-second decisions with life-altering implications; the choices made through extreme reliance on themselves and others allowed their lives to converge after the Holocaust and rebuild. In awe of the many miracles that led to his existence, their grandson compares, contrasts, and reflects on their life stories as he learns of them.

PIECING TOGETHER ACTS I, II, AND III

One more mishap and this book never happens.

If my grandparents' lives were classic three-act plays, then pre-World War II and the encroaching antisemitism set the stage in Act I; the second act entailed the harrowing traumas of the war and the subplots of how they survived. As my brother and I pieced together the bits of information that rolled our way over time, we realized we had landed squarely in the middle of Act III, when our grandparents chose to forge on and move their life drama along. We lacked the full context of the life dramas that led to our existence. We knew little of the dangers they faced at every turn, the split-second decisions with life-altering implications they were forced into making and what motivated them to rebuild with purpose. My parents knew some of Act I but little of Act II. Not that it was their fault: my parents were deliberately shielded from knowing too much as part of my grandparents' strategy for coping with their own turbulent histories.

As a child, I knew my grandparents all had a past they didn't like to talk about. I was okay with not knowing too much at the time. They all doted on my brother and me in their own ways, so I had no reason to press the issue. Their perseverance and gritty effort succeeded in ensuring that their first-generation American grandchildren didn't feel like "greeners," so much so that we had no clue how thoroughly they had achieved the American dream. We were just glad to share in that dream, happily living in rosier times without fully understanding how close our grandparents' nightmarish past loomed.

What follows are thoughts, memories, and stories told to me, witnessed by me, or both, representing a trajectory that has added a texture to my life for which I am forever proud and grateful. While personal, they are also communal in the sense that lessons of Jewish history and the individuals who comprise that history tell a tale of remarkable resilience and survival with purpose.

I tell their story as I learned it, over the course of several decades, eventually becoming part of their story.

FOUR SURVIVOR GRANDPARENTS

Intro to their Names
"Nana and Papa," "Grandma and Grandpa"

In America, Joachim "Romek" and Sala Wimmer became known as Jack and Sally Wimmer; Shaya and Feigele Szlas became Sam and Fay Schloss. How my mother's parents, the Wimmers, decided on Nana and Papa while my father's parents, the Schlosses, chose Grandma and Grandpa is a mystery of my youth I'll never solve. I know that both sets of grandparents wore those titles proudly. Throughout their lives, they were known by several different names, as will be seen in these pages.

Although he almost always wore a tie and had a formal air about him, Papa (Chaim Avraham Wimmer, aka Jack Wimmer, aka Joachim Wimmer, aka Romek Wimmer, aka Dr. Wimmer, aka Mr. Wimmer) was fun-loving, mischievous, creative, and friendly. Papa achieved legendary status (at least within dental circles) as a founder in the field of dental implantology. I didn't think much of the weird-looking widgets in his office or the gory dental slides he proudly projected on the wall as he practiced his lectures. The odd-shaped blades, screws, and porcelain frankly were not that exciting to a kid. However, seeing Papa passionately describe the dental conventions when he lectured members of his field and presented his wares was like watching an elite athlete give a post-performance interview. He gave it his all, and he was thankful for the opportunity. He took care of his business, and his business took care of him. After all, everyone has teeth and is a potential customer.

Jack Wimmer at his office desk at 19 West 34th St, NYC, photos of Dr. Leonard Linkow (pioneer of dental implantology) in background

While he loved implantology, the love of his life was his family. Foremost was Nana (Chaya Sara Wimmer, aka Sally Wimmer, aka Sala Wimmer). Nana was always by Papa's side as a loving foil. She continues to share her life wisdom and sharp insight with her children, grandchildren, great-grandchildren and great-great granddaughter.

Grandpa (Sam Schloss aka Shaya/Shayek Szlas) and Grandma (Fay Schloss aka Feigele/Fela Schloss) were always a bit more reserved. My guess as to how they chose Grandma and Grandpa is that they opted for the most typical American moniker possible as a proud sign that they had made it in the New World.

Grandpa, a painter by trade, always had his ladder, tarps, and some paint cans in the back of his brown station wagon. Grandpa was meticulous in everything he did. This trait served him well at work (and throughout his life). Sometimes he was gruff, but he was always happy to come over with Grandma and just be with us (or for us to visit their Bronx apartment). Grandma was the gentlest person I've ever met. She could cook a feast like it was no big deal; one of her greatest joys was feeding me and my brother (and eventually our first cousin, Emily – her only granddaughter). Grandma seemed so happy to just sit with us at the table and watch us eat. Her quiet enjoyment of feeding a third generation poignantly defied the cruel captors who had subjected her to forced starvation. I don't know if she ever consciously put it that way; we just felt unconditional love and had no reason to question why she was so quiet.

Nana and Papa were always more outgoing, Grandma and Grandpa more reserved. Nana and Papa would take us to the circus; Grandma and Grandpa liked to feed us and otherwise marvel at us being us. (Not that we were anything special). My brother and I were largely oblivious to the deeper common denominator between our two sets of survivor grandparents; we represented a cherished victory of sorts. The magnitude of what they lost and what they won became known to only us as we reached adulthood.

The 'Young' Dentist
Jack Wimmer's Office, 1995

Two prominent Italian dentists had just been given a spirited guided tour of the history of dental implants in an office across the street from the Empire State Building. There were the molds from the monkeys who were among the first recipients of dental implants. There were all types of dated blades, screws, and other dental doodads that are only interesting to those in the business. These artifacts told the origin story of the obscure concept of giving people a new set of permanent teeth instead of dentures. By the 1990s, some companies were even marketing dental implants as if they were inevitable – first you have baby teeth, then adult teeth, and then implants. But it was not always so accepted. It took lots of trial and error to perfect the tools and techniques that eventually became mainstream: safely cutting into otherwise healthy gums, inserting metal into the jaw, and affixing prosthetic teeth on top instead of dentures became mainstream.

To dentists who routinely inserted implants using the most modern tools and techniques, getting a tour of Park Dental Research Corp's office in New York City at 19 West 34th Street was like modern-day baseball players seeing Babe Ruth's old glove and wool uniform up close. There was something awesome about seeing how things used to be done that gave context to the dentists' craft. Oral surgeons who wield specialized screws would see the old blade implants they replaced and think, "How quaint!" It's like seeing a pair of George Washington's wooden teeth at the Smithsonian.

The tour guide in the sharp charcoal suit, red power tie, and European accent was Jack Wimmer, my Papa, president and founder of Park Dental. He excitedly explained model after model and capped off the tour with a demonstration of the plasma glow discharge system used to sterilize blades and other equipment.

"Any questions, gentlemen?"

They asked some technical questions about placements and techniques.

Jack answered with precision and showed clear mastery of his trade. He exuded the energy of a man much younger.

When they sated their professional curiosity, someone had one more question. "How old are you?" asked one of the Italian dentists in nervous wonderment, not wanting to insult.

"I am 50 years old," Jack said confidently with raised eyebrows and a satisfied grin. He was not 50. He was 72. He let his answer sink in as he saw them struggle to fathom it. Jack's eyes twinkled as he shrugged humbly and explained his answer to the curious dentists. "It is 50 years since I was liberated from camp; God gave me a second chance to live, and I do my best, so I try."

Jack used this line many times with different people over the years, changing only the number of years since he was liberated from a German work camp.

Sam Schloss
An Independent at Senior Living, 2015

The aides who worked with individual residents at Grandpa Sam Schloss's assisted living facility loved him. The staff? It depended. Sam sharply observed everything that went on at the beautifully manicured facility – and understood when things were good and when corners were being cut. He kept staff on their toes by not-so-shyly making his observations known. Sam's fantastic aide, Kathy, worked only part-time. Ever resourceful, Sam would often rely on some of the other residents' aides to help him when Kathy was off duty. Eye drops at night or the occasional assist at a meal were routine. Sam also made friends with aides who were interested in a few bucks on the side.

Sam's beloved Fay (Feigele) died a few years before his move to assisted living – or as he put it, "God's waiting room." Feigele was elegant, gentle, quiet, and unassuming. Sam used to joke that he was the opposite of Feigele and missed her terribly. "I married a refined city girl; see how beautiful she was?" he would sometimes ask as he would show someone his flip phone. "For a country bumpkin like me, I was very lucky." Sam's son, Bruce, had set the flip phone so Feigele's photo would appear every time Sam picked it up and opened it. Sam never got used to her not being by his side and often spoke to her at night.

During the day, though, he was constantly angling – whether it was to get a good table at dinner, a seat in a good card game, or fresher food. Of course, even though the tables and food were mostly decent and the card games were dicey enough for an assisted living facility, he always tried to see if he could do better. He couldn't help it.

Sam was not shy and would often make a beeline toward the owners when he had a chance to speak his mind. For instance, Sam cornered the owner and his son just as they entered the dining room during one particularly less-than-stellar dinner. After getting their attention and striking up a casual conversation, he started searching his pockets for something. They continued pleasantries but couldn't avoid noticing Sam's curious gestures. Pants and jacket pockets – nothing. Shirt pocket – nope. They switched gears. "Are you okay, Mr. Schloss?"

Finally, Sam reached into his jacket's inner breast pocket and pulled out a small bottle of pills and showed it to the owners. "Tell me what I want to know: do you know what this is?" he asked rhetorically.

The owners looked at each other quizzically. "Your medication, Mr. Schloss?" They didn't realize they had just taken the bait and were about to be reeled in.

Sam inched a bit closer as he went in for the kill. "That's right," Sam said as he held up the bottle proudly and moved it straight toward their eyes, keeping it directly in their line of vision as he spoke. "These are my pills," he said, as if explaining to a young child. "Which I'm supposed to take." He infected his voice upward and slowly inched the bottle closer to their faces. "With food." Ever closer and a little louder. "That I can eat!" Now showing them the instructions that he was supposed to take the drugs with food, he said,

"Please, you know I'm a survivor; can you at least get me some fresh bread?"

Point made.

A few aides looking on chuckled out loud, wishing they had their cellphones on hand to record what they had just seen. The aides had observed that the bread was not always fresh, too, but no one had the nerve to make the case for change quite that way. Only Sam could pull that off, and some of the aides and residents enjoyed watching the drama play out.

To be fair, Sam's beloved Fay was a phenomenal cook and, even when she could no longer cook, he knew his way around the kitchen and made his own delicious meals. Nothing can compare to homemade. Thankfully, the owners took the biting yet constructive criticism in stride and did their best to spruce things up for Sam. Sam's eagle eye and sensitivity to a certain standard kept them on their toes.

Sally Wimmer
Friday afternoon, 2023

"Hello, Jonathan?"

"How did you know it was me, Nana?"

"My heart told me so. You never miss a 'Good Shabbos' call."

The typical beginning of many Friday afternoon phone calls.

After she asks about my week, I ask about hers.

Nonchalantly, she often says things like, "Well, I went to a doctor this week and I took an injection in the eye."

Wait, what? Did she actually just tell me that she received a needle in the eye? "Nana, are you okay? Did it hurt?"

"One, two, three, a little pressure and that's it. I have to be able to read, you know that."

That's true. Nana spends her days praying from the *siddur* [Hebrew prayer book], reciting *Tehillim* [psalms], reading articles and books, and watching the news. The thought of curtailing that routine in any way is nothing compared to a little needle in the eye.

"I was watching the news the other day and it was so aggravating," she says. "Did you hear about...?" A synopsis of the vexing news of the day comes next.

"Nana, if it's so aggravating, why not watch less news and say a few more chapters of Tehillim?"

Without missing a beat, Nana says something like, "I have to watch; I have to know what I'm saying Tehillim for, right?"

Touché.

Grandma, Fay Schloss
North Miami Beach, 1987

On my first solo visit on winter break to Grandma and Grandpa's, I woke up to a continental breakfast of nice dairy dishes. Not exactly the bowl of cereal I preferred, but at 14, I understood enough that Grandma was thoroughly enjoying the whole experience of me eating her food in her kitchen. I gladly partook. Without my asking, Grandma poured me a cup of milk.

"Thank you, Grandma." Again, not my usual routine, but I decided I'd drink it anyway. As I was reaching for the cup, Grandma started pouring me a second cup. My puzzlement shone through; I didn't have to ask why she was doing it.

"This way, you shouldn't have to pour twice when you want more, *Tatele* [little Daddy, a term of endearment]," she said with a huge smile, using a Yiddish term of endearment. I dutifully appreciated every ounce and morsel. At the time, it was hard to understand why drinking two cups of milk appeared to give Grandma such pleasure. Of course, there were times when she did not have such luxuries or anything beyond stale scraps and bread and water. She rarely spoke about those times whose weight informed her daily life. Doting on an appreciative grandson? Absolutely priceless to Grandma.

A Strange Word

I first heard the term Holocaust when I was about eight. Nana and Papa were going to a Holocaust memorial and used the term in a solemn way that struck me as unusual. The relatively somber aura and mood produced by that one word contrasted with Nana and Papa's usual cheerful dispositions. I asked my main source of information – my brother Daniel – what it meant.

Daniel, all of three and a half years older than me (but wiser than his years), gave me the basics to satisfy my curiosity. "That's when people who didn't like Jews in Europe decided to stop shopping in Jewish stores, threw rocks in their windows, and did other mean things to Jews." He knew more than he was letting on, of course, but did not want to burden his little brother with too many details.

I remember thinking, "Why would people, for no apparent reason, be so mean to Jews?" Did any of my grandparents' families have stores? (Yes, they did.) Are we anywhere near Europe? (No.) Did they have any windows broken? (Yes.) What "other mean things" happened? (Plenty.) It sounded horrible, but I did not press for more answers then. Too scary.

I was satisfied with Daniel's answer in that I thought I understood why the usually boisterous Nana and Papa seemed unusually sad when the word Holocaust came up. I'd seen a window break by accident before. The thought of glass breaking was jarring, messy, noisy, and dangerously hard to clean up. My eight-year-old self tried to imagine why people would deliberately inflict that on anyone else.

Homework Assignment

When I was in fourth grade (about ten years old), I came home from my Jewish Day School with an assignment that forced me to revisit the issue: "If any of your grandparents are survivors, or if you know any survivors, ask them to fill out this form." My brother received the same assignment.

It was a blank chart with a few columns – Name, Relation, Age at Death, Place of Death – listed at the top with dark black lines to be filled in underneath. The assignment was a bit blunt for a ten-year-old. In the days before Microsoft Excel, this strange spreadsheet's stark columns looked more like a form to fill out in a doctor's office than a tool to foster a dialog. So, I brought the form home and asked my mom to help me fill it out. I don't remember exactly how it got filled out, but it did. To my surprise, after a day or two of hushed phone calls and in-person conversations, a few dozen names appeared on the charts. My grandparents listed their parents, some grandparents, brothers, sisters, cousins, uncles, and aunts – relatives whose lives were all cut short and were now being given a cameo role in a fourth-grader's homework.

The gravity was lost upon me at the time. But I sensed that our innocent inquiry for help with some homework had gently touched, and perhaps helped to soothe, our grandparents' raw nerves somewhat, Papa and Nana especially. They went over each name with me. "These were my two younger sisters, Shifra and Toba," Nana said as she recalled the innocent, loving girls. "This was my younger brother, Salomon – Shlomo, like you." Papa told me that part of my Hebrew name was after his younger brother, who was named after their grandfather, Solomon Wimmer.

My father had to get the information for the homework chart from Grandma and Grandpa for us – it was still too raw for them to discuss with their young grandsons, even in this context.

There were about 30 names of children, teenagers, young adults, middle-aged adults, and the elderly listed. Over time, I learned about many of the people on my homework list. Many of them appear in this book – lives cut short but purposefully remembered. I still have that chart and looked at it when discussing possible names for my children with my wife.

My grandparents rarely, if ever, spoke about their experiences with my parents and uncles when they were young. Outwardly, they focused on caring for and raising children. Career and community came next in varying degrees. Normalcy – that's what they wanted for their children. In keeping things normal, though, they fiercely shielded their American children from being burdened with the personal horror stories of World War II Europe. Sharing bad memories with their children? Never. Way too raw. No need to scare the children as they were building normal lives in a new, free world. In the 1950s and 1960s, they lived their American dreams by keeping their European nightmares at bay. However, those nightmares never go away. Like a scene in a rearview mirror, the memories loomed closer than they appeared on the surface. To cope with the past, they keenly focused on building futures. How they dealt with and confronted them has impacted generations.

Prewar Small-Town Life
Shaya Szlas/Sam Schloss

Grandpa Sam grew up in Jasieniec, a small town in northeastern Poland. Shaya, as his parents called him, was the third of four children born to Jacob and Miriam Schloss. Sam revered his parents and clung to their memory. The abrupt separation from them and his siblings when he was 20 left him alone in the world with only himself and his wits to rely upon. Sam would always describe his parents with awe tinged with self-deprecation. "My dear father loved to read books and to study Talmud, the opposite of myself," Sam would recall with a slight chuckle. Sam's father, Jacob, was from Długosiodło, a town near Jasiniec near the Russian border. Jacob had spent his late teenage years at the famous Slonim Yeshiva, where he acquired a love of Jewish learning. He learned how to perform *shechita* – the ritual slaughter of cows and chickens and how to prepare them according to Jewish law and tradition. Blessed with a beautiful voice, Jacob studied *chazzones* [Jewish liturgy] at a cantorial school in Berlin before World War I. Jacob also learned how to read music, sing from notes, and play the clarinet at the cantorial school. As a shochet and *chazzan* [cantor], Jacob would always be able to find work where Jews lived. Shortly after returning to Poland from Berlin, Jacob's musical training came in handy; he was conscripted to the Russian army and landed a plum position in the military orchestra as a clarinet player. Jacob was discharged from the army shortly before World War I. "After my dear father came back from the Russian army, he was set up with many different girls; he was a good catch – not so much like me, a country bumpkin who got lucky finding a beautiful city girl like Mom," Sam recalled.

Jacob and Miriam married in 1915 in Jasiniec and lived with Miriam's family. Miriam's father, Avraham Y'shaya Mishler, ran a *kretchma* [tavern] in town and helped manage a Polish landowner's livestock transactions. He also bought milk and dairy products, which he sold in city markets. The family huddled together as best as possible as World War I wreaked havoc. "The Polish army, having many antisemite high-ranking officers in their army, used to come to villages where Jews were living and do what they wanted; soldiers would rob, rape, and beat up Jews for fun," Sam said. His parents' first few years of marriage were fraught with worry about the haphazard violence that could erupt at any moment. When Poland won its independence in 1918 and Marshal Józef Piłsudski came to power, things quieted down for Polish Jewry. Piłsudski advocated for judging people not by ethnicity but by loyalty to the state. And the Jews were loyal. So Piłsudski helped protect the Jews.

Though things improved for Poland's Jews, Jacob and Miriam understood the ugliness that lay just beneath the surface of the state-imposed easing of hostility toward Jews.

Avraham Yishaya passed away in 1922, shortly before Sam was born. Sam's Hebrew name was Avraham Yishaya – "Shaya" was a riff off his grandfather's longer name.

At five years old, Jacob started teaching Shaya to read the Hebrew alphabet. At six, Shaya started public school and continued his religious training with his father in the afternoons. That was the plan, at least. Shaya's classmates harassed the only Jew in their class mercilessly as Piłsudski's tolerance did not trickle down to the masses. "*Zhid!* Christ-killer!" they yelled. Shaya's classmates barely understood what they were saying, but they said it with such gusto that Shaya was constantly on edge.

(Decades later, half a world away, similar sentiment bubbled up into schools, including on many prestigious college campuses. "Zionists! Baby-killers! By all means necessary!" These and other antisemitic canards rang loud across the quads of Harvard University, Columbia University, and the University of Pennsylvania, to name a few. But in the ivory towers of the Ivy League, these antisemitic bigots were targeting other college students and some professors who dared to be Jewish on campus. Sam faced hate at a much younger age.)

"To hate a Jew, the Polish children learned at home from their parents and in church from the priest," Sam later recalled. The vile name-calling and frequent beatdowns were not exactly an ideal learning environment. That's a lot for a second grader to endure daily. After second grade, Jacob and Miriam took the family for a summer vacation to Komarów, where Miriam's sister, Esther, lived with her husband, Jack Fleischer. Jack and Esther owned and ran the general store in Komarów. They had no children of their own but had taken in Shaya's cousin, Goldy, to live with them. Why not one more? Aunt Esther loved children and was sad to hear about Shaya's schooling. Komarów was approximately 50 percent Jewish and had plenty of kids Shaya's age running around. Esther invited Shaya to stay with them, and he readily accepted. The prospect of not being the only Jew in class was a huge relief, even though schooling would occupy his entire day.

As public school was not yet in session, the *Rebbe* [rabbi] suggested that Shaya attend cheder (Jewish school) full-time until public school started. Cheder was open from morning until suppertime, with a one-hour break for lunch and a few sessions of recess to play outside in the fresh air. "To be honest, I didn't enjoy the studies too much, but I enjoyed the group of Jewish boys; I felt a big difference learning in a class with my own than learning in a class with a bunch of Jew-haters."

Wimmer Family in Wieliczka

The Wimmers lived in a six-family home in Wieliczka (pronounced Vee-yel-ICH-ka), a suburb of Kraków near Poland's famous salt mines. A balcony with wrought iron railings with the initials SW and GW ensconced in a crest overlooked a large town square where Polish merchants would come two or three times each week to peddle their wares. (If you check Google Earth, SW and GW can still be seen on those railings.)

The Wimmer Home

Nachum Wimmer was the gatekeeper of sorts who organized the marketplace for the municipality and registered each merchant. Nachum's father, Solomon Wimmer, was originally from Vienna. He was an architect and a builder who came to Wieliczka in the late 19th century from Klasno. Solomon built many of the municipal buildings in and around Wieliczka. He also built a home for his family in the corner of the town square and put his initials and his wife Gittel's on the balconies' railings. Up the block, he built the *Bais Midrash Dorshei Tov* [House of Learning of the Seekers of Good], a study hall/synagogue. Solomon also delivered chemicals, timber, and lumber to the nearby salt mines and even served on the local town council. Nachum continued in these businesses and the Wimmers lived fairly comfortably.

Young Romek Wimmer

Nachum and Serkei (née Palak) Wimmer endearingly called their oldest son Romek. Although his Hebrew name was Chaim Avraham, "Romek," a shortened version of a nickname for Avraham (Avromek) rolled off the tongue easily. Romek naturally liked shortcuts (or, said differently, the most efficient way of doing something), as even his name was a nickname of a nickname. My Papa enjoyed being a wise guy, testing the limits of authority while also respecting it. He playfully wrestled and fought with his brothers Elkan Hirsh (Henyek) and Solomon (named for the grandfather) as their little sister Sheva (Sabina) watched in amusement.

Public school until midday, followed by a quick lunch and cheder in the afternoons, filled the Wimmer children's days. Romek was one of four Jews in his public school class. He got along well enough with his classmates, but he was not entirely comfortable. Romek and his three friends did not attend public school on Saturdays or Jewish holidays. That alone would have made them stand out. Romek's mother parlayed what could have been a precarious academic and social situation into an opportunity. Romek would go to one of his Polish classmates' houses on Sunday afternoon to catch up on what he had missed, always with fruits or other goodies from the marketplace. On Christmas, Romek would deliver a big strudel, a challah, and fish, ensuring that the classmate would readily share notes and homework. While Romek regularly heard antisemitic comments in school and felt their ugly undertones percolating around him, the flow of small gifts paved the way for Romek's schooling to remain largely unaffected by the wave that would soon envelope Wieliczka and beyond.

Keep the Kid Busy (with Teeth)!

"Fire! Fire!" Romek screamed as he ran from the stairwell into the courtyard in front of his home. Everyone ran outside. The whole town heard the ruckus of firefighters coming to put out a blaze near the front stairwell of the Wimmer home. A petrified Romek watched from afar from his neighbors' grocery store as firefighters extinguished the flames and remained afraid even after the fire was put out. Romek was thankful that the fire caused only minimal damage and hurt no one, but he imagined his parents would come down hard on him for playing with sparklers indoors – if they ever found out. Romek had carefully lit a sparkler with a friend and, not so carefully, threw the match toward the bottom of the steps right next to where the hay used to warm the house was stored. Oops. Romek felt bad but said nothing to anyone. He saw a police investigator talking to his father outside the front door. "Looks like one of the bricks came off the chimney and sparked a fire down here, Mr. Wimmer." Romek bit his tongue hard as his father nodded in disappointment at the poor quality of workmanship on the chimney. Romek clutched his chest as he thanked God quietly for the investigator's incompetence. As he did so, he felt the matchbook in his shirt pocket – and promptly flushed it down the toilet.

Romek's father accepted the investigator's findings. Romek's mother, however, suspected that her eldest son was a more likely culprit than the chimney brick. She sensed his fear and never confronted him about it as she understood that his distress was punishment enough.

"We have to keep him busy, Nachum," she said. "He's going to try more daring things."

Nachum Wimmer's brother in Belgium practiced dentistry. In midsummer 1936, Nachum and Serkei took their family to Belgium to visit for a couple of weeks. Romek bonded with his cousins, who taught him how to mix plasters in their father's dental practice. Fun stuff for a preteen. The process fascinated Romek – the feel of the plaster at the beginning through the fashioning of the end product; it was an exciting arts-and-crafts activity that served a real purpose. The usually rambunctious, jumpy Romek focused attentively as his cousins and uncle showed him how to use plasters.

Not long after the fire in the stairwell, Nachum and Serkei remembered Romek's atypical, focused interest in Belgium and reached out to Wieliczka dentist Dr. Maximillian Schlang. Dr. Schlang *davened* [prayed] at Bais Midrash Dorshei Tov and well understood Romek – a good-natured kid who lacked *zitzfleisch* [literally, skin on the bottom, figuratively meaning the ability to stay focused on something for extended periods]. Sitting still in school, for instance, was challenging for Romek. Nonetheless, Romek's natural charm with people of all ages in *shul* [synagogue] made Dr. Schlang's decision to take on a part-time apprentice easier and less of a professional risk.

Dr. Schlang ran a state-of-the-art dental office using relatively new innovations in dentistry such as Novocaine, which softened patients' pain, and porcelain jacket crowns, which covered and protected the entire surface of a tooth. Romek watched Dr. Schlang and particularly enjoyed helping out with tooth extractions. Dr. Schlang appreciated Romek's laser-focused interest in his processes and procedures and rewarded his young apprentice with an experience that would never fly elsewhere. Sometimes, when the patient was either in so much pain or too high on laughing gas to notice, Dr. Schlang let Romek pull teeth.

While he could not always sit as a student in school, Romek patiently reveled in the art of using his hands to help people with their teeth. On top of keeping the fidgety teen occupied, something else about Dr. Schlang's office piqued Romek's interest – Dr. Schlang never lacked for patients. The fact that everyone has teeth represented a limitless market for customers. Even as Romek appreciated the business side of dental practice, he had no idea how fortunate he was to be interning in such a hands-on way in Eastern Europe in 1938. As Romek was learning to pull teeth in Poland, Jews in Germany and Austria were being squeezed out of dentistry and other skilled professions.

In 1935, the Nuremberg Laws in effect in Germany forbade Jews from obtaining dental licenses. By 1938, the next stage of the Nuremberg laws stripped Jewish dentists in Germany and Austria of their licenses altogether. Reports about Germany's policies toward Jews trickled across the border, but Romek realized none of it. He focused on learning daily.

Other than perhaps lighting an internal flame of desire to run his own practice one day, Romek did not start any more fires. His mother's vision started to take root.

Shaya Growing Up in Ostrów Masowiecka

Shaya's parents had a cow and raised chickens. They had their own dairy and poultry and ran a small grocery store. Between the store and Jacob Schloss's cantorial gigs on the high holidays in the nearby city of Ostrów Masowiecka, Shaya's parents made a decent living, at least until Hitler came to power. Jacob and Miriam often let regular customers – non-Jew and Jew alike – keep tabs at the store if they expressed a need. Even so, as far as Grandpa Shaya remembered, there was always an undercurrent of tension with his family's non-Jewish neighbors. Early on, it was mostly manifested in school. Kids would say things they had heard at home or in church and then haze Shaya. He numbed himself to the name-calling and the occasional beatdowns. Being the only Jew in class was not comfortable.

Shaya's father subscribed to some weekly Jewish newspapers and listened to crackly radio reports about the goings-on in Germany. The passage and implementation of the Nuremberg Laws in Germany were worrisome but largely did not impact Shaya's community at first. Occasionally, German Jews fleeing eastward passed through town and told stories of rampant, unpredictable violence against them.

That's when the hazing spread from the schoolyard to the marketplace. Emboldened by news from Germany, the local non-Jews began to boycott the Szlas' store. Then came the picketing. Ironically, the antisemites who boycotted and picketed the Szlas' store had also been customers. Like modern-day BDS (Boycott, Divestment, and Sanctions) advocates whose unadulterated Jew-hatred trumps practicality, the boycotters and picketers left themselves with no place to shop locally for groceries. The intensity of the picketers ebbed and flowed for a few weeks, making it increasingly difficult to run a store. They still had a few acres of land, some chickens, and a cow, so they made a go of operating despite local pressure to close. Jacob's brother Abraham had emigrated to the

United States in the late 1920s and sent some occasional support that helped keep Jacob and Miriam Szlas's family afloat.

The Non-Smiling Family Portrait

Author: Before going to sleep and dreaming of his dear Feigele while living at the senior living facility, Shaya wished his dear parents, grandmother, and siblings in a 1934 family portrait a good night, too. As touching as that may sound, the family portrait proudly placed on Shaya's night table next to his bed looked brooding. Shaya, approximately 12 years old in the photo, sat on the ground with his arms folded as if he had just been told to sit in a corner. Shaya and his parents, grandmother, sisters, brother, and first cousin were all dressed in their Shabbos-best clothing, though no one looked particularly pleased to be posing. We understood that this was the one prized photo of his family that somehow had survived the war. But why was everyone so dour?

Even amid the boycotts, a neighboring Polish family regularly came to the Szlas' grocery. The family did not participate in the protests and was generally polite – an anomaly among their neighbors. Jacob had extended credit to the family for extended periods without payment. Sporadic payments were better than none, and at least this family was respectful. One day, after adding a large order to their tab, the head of the family burst into the store with great news.

"Jacob, I'm settling up my whole tab today!"

"Thank you. Are you sure?"

"Oh yes. Definitely!"

As Jacob turned to retrieve his ledger of accounts receivable, the man said, "Oh, you don't need to get that, but you do need to get your family together."

"Excuse me?" asked a bewildered Jacob.

"I just bought a camera. I will take a photograph of your family," the man said, smiling and sure of himself.

"I thought you said you wanted to pay off the bill; if it's too much, I can continue to work with you."

"I said the bill is now paid off entirely; go get your family for a photo." His demeanor changed from jovial and loud to stern and softly menacing.

And that's why no one smiled in the 1934 Szlas family portrait.

Left to right: back row: Yitzchak Schloss, Paja Schloss, Sam Goldberg (first cousin – his mother Faiga and Miriam were sisters); second row: Shaina Rochel Mishler (Miriam and Faiga's mother), Miriam Mishler Schloss, Yaakov Schloss; Bottom row: Shaya Schloss and Clara Schloss. Of those in the picture, only Sam Goldberg and Shaya survived the Holocaust.

New Home, New Profession?

The Polish antisemites could not stomach that the Szlas' store was able to remain open despite their efforts to make it uncomfortable for the Jewish proprietors.

So they started a different method of intimidation. At nighttime, they sent rocks flying through the windows. Damage around the property became evident each morning. After dark, Shaya and his family dared not venture outside. One night, a rock through the window landed squarely on Shaya's mother's forehead. The wound required a hospital visit and stitches, but the rock left a gaping hole in more than just Miriam Szlas's forehead. The rock breached the security of home. The Szlas family braced themselves during the steady transition from tepid tolerance to intolerance where they had lived for decades. They even survived competition from the boycotters and picketers who eventually opened their own store. After the brick incident, Jacob nailed wooden boards to the window frames. However, the wooden boards had the opposite effect. It showed that Shaya's family felt threatened.

In late 1934, the antisemitic Poles decided to bargain from a position of strength and run the three Jewish families out of town for good. The Poles, who had most of the last year making their Jewish neighbors' lives miserable, apparently grew tired of their own shenanigans and simply wanted the Jews out. They approached each of the three Jewish families with an offer to purchase their properties. The alternative to taking the lowball price, of course, would have been escalation of the Poles' tactics. With reports of rampant beatdowns and worse from Germany, the bricks, boycotts, and protests were relatively tame. The Szlases and the other two Jewish families jointly decided to take the paltry offer for their land; they could not feasibly refuse it without risking their own safety in their hometown.

Shaya's family moved from the small village of Jasiniec, close to the Russian border, to the nearby city of Ostrów to the west, where there was a larger population of Jews. They rented a property with a storefront and an adjacent apartment, fixed it up, and set themselves up as storekeepers again. It was smaller than their original store, but they were able to sell milk, eggs, and other grocery items as they had in Jasiniec. It was enough to call home for Jacob and Miriam, their children, and Miriam's mother, Bubbe Shayne Ruchel.

After leaving behind the uncomfortable ordeals of Jasiniec, the Szlases found comfort and strength in numbers. The children had mostly Jewish friends and neighbors for a change and participated in Zionist youth organizations. Shaya and his sisters attended public school, though they had fewer confrontations with peers in Ostrów, while Shaya's older brother, Isaac, attended yeshiva in Warsaw. Though Isaac's yeshiva cost Miriam and Jacob money that they couldn't afford, they believed it important for their oldest son to continue his Jewish studies. Isaac had the aptitude and the attitude that Jacob saw Shaya lacked.

Jacob nonetheless tried to inspire Shaya and sat with him daily, engaged in religious studies. *Kol Yisrael yesh lahem chelek, l'olam haba* [all of Israel has a portion of the World to Come] Jacob tinged the learning with a singsong melody as he taught *Pirkei Avos* [Ethics of the Fathers] with his son. Though Shaya often sat with arms folded and may not have internalized everything, he could not help but sense the vigor with which his father tried to imbue him with Jewish knowledge and pride.

Shaya preferred spending time with the local Zionist youth group. In the evening, Ostrów's teens would meet in a hall with instructors, who showed movie reels about life on a kibbutz and talked up *Aliya* [moving to what is now Israel]. They'd sing, socialize, and play games – thankfully, a far cry from the tense days in the village of Jasiniec.

One of Shaya's friends from the Zionist youth group, a boy a year older than Shaya named Mordechai Zolzberg, bragged about apprenticing for a local tailor and encouraged his friend to follow suit. Everyone needs a good tailor. Shaya's parents were not thrilled with the idea of their son's newfound ambition. *"Est past nisht, Shaya* [It's beneath you, Shaya]." Wanting to join his cool older friend, Shaya lobbied his parents hard, and they relented. They reasoned: "He doesn't even have the patience to sit and learn without fidgeting for a few minutes; he's going to have the zitzfleish to sit and make suits?" But they relented. "Let him try. Okay, so a son wants to be a tailor – at least it's an honest living."

Mordechai Zolzberg set Shaya up with this boss, who gladly welcomed Shaya to his shop. With his friend Mordechai at his side after the hard-fought battle with his folks, Shaya excitedly started his apprenticeship. On day one, Shaya learned how to hold a needle and make stitches properly. He mastered holding the needle correctly and breezed through each stitch. Days two and day three – more of the same. "When do we make suits?" Shaya wanted to know. The next day, more of the same. For Shaya, the word "boredom" does not sufficiently describe learning to hold a needle and make the same stitch day after day. The tedious repetition made studying with his father seem exciting. Shaya could not understand Mordechai's enthusiasm for this tedious trade. By day four, Shaya quit – about one day later than his parents had expected.

Bubbe Shayna Rochel
Meriting Dignity

Shaya's grandmother, Shayna Rochel Mishler, lived with his family. She was a pious woman who spent her day reading psalms, cooking, and otherwise doing what she could to help out with her children's families. Decidedly old school, Bubbe Shayna Rochel did not tolerate disrespect well and sometimes threatened to hit misbehaving children with a wooden spoon. This, of course, led Shaya and his younger sister to come up with fun nicknames. They called their grandmother *Sheina Leffel* [sweet spoon] behind her back. "She was a little lady running after us with a big spoon," Shaya recalled. "We thought it was funny; my father didn't think it was so funny."

The pressures of moving around due to antisemitic threats weighed heavily on Shayna Rochel. She had been down that road before during World War I and sensed a massive nastiness overtaking the world. She focused her prayers on the health and safety of her children as she recited her daily psalms.

In mid-August 1939, war was looming. The news reports from Germany, especially for Jews, were grim. Bubbe Shayna Rochel worried about her children, grandchildren, and great-grandchildren who would have to fight the Nazis. Thinking about it gave her palpitations. She went out for some fresh air and fed the chickens. No use. No amount of fresh air could overcome the suffocating foreboding she sensed. She went to bed, had a heart attack, and died a few hours later. As per Jewish custom, the family buried Bubbe Shayna Rochel within the next 24 hours in Ostrów's Jewish cemetery. Her family sat a full seven days of shiva in mourning. Bubbe Shayna Rochel may have been the last Jew in Poland to have had that privilege for quite some time.

War Comes to Shaya's Family in Ostrów
German Degradation Begins

On a clear, beautiful Friday morning, bombs rained down on Ostrów courtesy of the German air force. Hours later, German soldiers marched into town. Shaya's family huddled together in their boarded home and peeked through windows. They could only hope the storm would soon pass. The Germans looked so strong and organized as they marched through. Gunshots and screams sporadically marked the day. By nightfall, as Shabbos began, the Germans had set up camp in the city and helped themselves to Jewish homes. Looting, rapes, killing – all of Bubbe Shayna Rochel's nightmares were playing out. The two shuls had their Torahs and other holy books torn, burned, and strewn about. German efficiency was on full display – trucks pulled up to Jewish-owned stores and warehouses and their contents were promptly emptied in an organized and efficient manner, even with the frenzied pace.

By Sunday morning, things quieted down until the early afternoon when German soldiers walked through town barking with loudspeakers and repeating:

"All men 15 and above, report to the high school soccer stadium. *Schnell* [Quick]!"

As Jacob readied to go, he and Miriam looked at each other and then at 16-year-old Shaya. "You stay here. Nothing good is coming of this," Jacob said. So Shaya hid with his mother and sister in the attic while Jacob represented the family at the soccer field.

As the throngs of men crowded the streets heading in one direction, Jacob prayed to the One Above.

At the soccer field, the Nazis had set up a large platform with a speaker's stand. Several German soldiers with machine guns herded the masses to the middle of the field and then surrounded them. Randomly, soldiers plucked a few Jews with long beards, *payos* [sidelocks], and *tzitzis* [fringes] from the crowd and shoved them up to the platform. The Germans entertained themselves by cutting the Jews' beards and making them pose in different demeaning ways as a punctilious German photographer documented the spectacle. The Germans genuinely enjoyed this grotesque bullying, knowing it would impact all assembled at the expense of the few selected. The Germans forced everyone to stand and watch to demoralize, dehumanize, and instill fear. After a few hours, the Germans grew tired of it and then barked some new rules to the gathered:

"You are under curfew. No one may be in the street after dark. If even one German is harmed or disrespected, your whole city will suffer! Tomorrow, open your stores and go about your normal business." The incongruity was striking and intimidating in and of itself. On the one hand, they were imposing stark restrictions with vague but fearsome consequences; on the other hand, they were issuing a directive to return to business as usual, albeit with the same vague and fearsome consequences for noncompliance.

By the time the Germans delivered the new ground rules and told those gathered to go home, the sun had set. The Jews were all in violation of curfew! The crowd that had shuffled into the soccer field lethargically earlier that day scattered immediately as they ran home with bullets and evil laughter flying all around. Not everyone dodged the Nazi bullets that night. Hiding in the attic a few blocks away, Shaya heard the tumult of the screams and flurry of sporadic gunfire and felt guilty for letting his father go without him. He silently cursed the Nazis and prayed for his father's safe return. Jacob, thankful that Shaya was hiding safely in the attic, made it home in one piece.

On Monday morning, the Szlases opened the grocery store as per orders. In anticipation of some unwanted visitors later, they hid some of the better merchandise. When soldiers came and helped themselves, there was not much to steal from this pathetic little grocery. Late in the day, two German gendarmes came in and looked around. Finding little to take, they turned their attention to Jacob's cap. "Nice Jew hat," one said of the little black cap that most of the Jews in Ostrów wore. One of them grabbed it off his head, hoping to instigate a fight, and examined it as Jacob stood stoically, bracing himself for the worst. As he handed the hat back to Jacob, the German got up in Jacob's face as if daring him to punch. "The Russians will be coming here soon; aren't you happy about that?" They were referring to the Hitler-Stalin Non-Aggression Pact. Officially, it was an agreement between Nazi Germany and the

Soviet Union in which the two countries agreed to divide Poland between them and refrain from taking any military action against the other. As history showed, Hitler used it as a tool to dupe the Soviets into sitting back and allowing Germany to encroach on Poland, closer to the Russian border, without any serious threat.

Jacob looked straight ahead and answered calmly: "We Jews are loyal people; it does not matter who governs us. We will respect their laws." It was not what Jacob said, but how he said it, that defused the situation. Jacob resolutely opted not to take the bait when provoked, so the German gendarmes moved on.

For two weeks, the Szlases endured these tense encounters. Eventually, there was nothing left to steal.

The German gendarmes had miscalculated; though Ostrów was only a few miles from the Russian border, Ostrów stayed in German hands and Jews were ordered to leave, not the reverse.

As Polish people could freely move from the Russian zone to the German zone, Miriam Szlas dressed as a Polish woman to scout for a place to settle in their old village of Jasiniec, situated in the Russian zone.

Scapegoating Then and Now

Those who stayed in Ostrów – mostly those who had not been able or were unwilling to leave their homes and businesses to cross over to the Soviet side – paid dearly. In early November 1939, a German soldier set fire to a wooden house in the center of town and allowed it to quickly spread. The Germans did not allow the fire to be put out until many buildings had burned down. They compounded their own wickedness by cynically blaming the Jews themselves for the fire. They chose to scapegoat a Jewish owner of a local brewery. The poor Jew was killed and hanged in a prominent spot in the town square with a sign placed on him that read: "This is the Jew who burned down the town." The targets of this sick, twisted marketing ploy were those local non-Jews who may still have had a semblance of sympathy toward their Jewish neighbors. If Jews would haphazardly destroy the town, the logic went, then they probably deserved whatever the Germans had in store for them. The Germans sought to fan the flames of enmity so no one would think twice about providing Jews any solace.

Author: Though decades apart and a continent away, Jew-hating Hamas used this same playbook in October 2023. They launched a missile toward Israel, but it landed in a Gaza hospital parking lot, killing several people. Rather than admit their own atrocity of targeting Israeli civilians with rocket fire, Hamas immediately accused Israel of targeting a hospital and wantonly killing hundreds. Utilizing the speed and breadth of internet access to fuel a false narrative, Hamas succeeded in instigating riots against Jews and Israel that erupted worldwide. Though the story was debunked as an errant missile launched from within Gaza intended for Israel, the deceitful marketing arguably did more damage around the world than the crude missile could have done had it actually reached its target. German Propaganda Minister Josef Goebbels would have been proud.

In one of the first organized massacres of Jews in wartime Europe, the SS rounded up all Jewish men, forcing them into the cellars at the city jail and the ice cellar of the local brewery on trumped-up charges of being complicit in arson. The next day, November 11, 1939, the SS forced the men onto trucks. They were driven to the southern end of the town, stripped naked, and ordered to dig a large pit. The SS machine-gunned all but six of them. Th e six remaining Jews were then forced to throw the other bodies into the pit and cover it with a little earth, followed by an order to pour lime over the bodies.

Ostrów's Jewish women and children were brought out next and the gruesome scene repeated itself. By the next morning, the exhausted and traumatized six surviving men finished their forced macabre labor and they, too, were killed. Proud of their work, the SS documented the gruesome slaughter with precise records and photos. On display at the US Holocaust Museum in Washington, D.C., is a photograph of a Nazi soldier standing next to an elderly man at the edge of a pit with the caption "The Last Victim." (According to German records accompanying that photograph, 364 men, women, and children were executed by the 4th Police Battalion, commanded by Police Colonel Brenner.)

Months earlier, it would have been hard to imagine that moving back to the antisemitic village of Jasiniec near the Russian border would be the lesser of two evils. As uncomfortable as it may have been to move back to Jasiniec, the decision spared the Szlas family from the pit on the outskirts of Ostrów.

Emboldened Antisemitism Reaches the Wimmer Family in Wieliczka

In 1938, Germany passed a series of laws aimed at separating Jews from the rest of the population. One such law was enacted in August 1938 when authorities decreed that by January 1, 1939, Jewish men and women with "non-Jewish" name origins had to add "Israel" and "Sara," respectively, to their names on their passports. A month or so later, Jews' passports were decreed invalid unless branded with a red capital J stamp. The locals who had boycotted the Szlases' grocery in Ostrów were simply following the lead of those in power. Antisemitic legislation emboldened the masses, who didn't necessarily need formal government approval to act on their antisemitic feelings; the legislation just made it more socially acceptable. If Kristallnacht (Night of Broken Glass, when Jewish stores and synagogues across Germany were destroyed on the night of November 9-10, 1938) made it official that Germany had decided to terrorize its Jewish citizens to the fullest, the laws leading up to it were like a heavy door that had been set in motion to close out their freedoms. For instance, if Jews and their property were, with Germany's explicit permission, ripe for the taking in Germany, why should Poland's non-Jews be left out of the fun?

It was this mentality that led to local Poles' Andikes (Ahn-di-kez), boycotts of Jewish businesses. By 1938, the boycotts hit Wieliczka, too. Wieliczka, where Jews and non-Jews got along and did business in and near its famous salt mines. Wieliczka, the Kraków suburb where Nachum Wimmer's father, Solomon, had designed and built the municipal buildings and the several multifamily buildings that formed the town square – the place for farmers to sell their produce and wares. By the late 1930s, Wieliczka was no longer hospitable to Jews, or the Wimmer family in particular. Nachum had to relinquish his position as the gatekeeper of the municipal concession stands which his father had set up to non-Jewish neighbors.

A local fascist party got a law passed to outlaw shechita. The invasion of the local government into religious freedoms, to perform ritual slaughter, worried some of the Jews of Wieliczka enough to make them leave, or at least think about leaving. Who knew what might come next? More ridiculous laws? But where were things better? Every Jewish household in Wieliczka grappled with those questions. Some fled to Kraków; perhaps there would be strength in numbers in the bigger city nearby. Others went to other cities. Some stayed put, preferring the familiarity of home, however uncomfortable at the moment, over an unknown.

So long as Dr. Schlang remained willing and so long as Romek remained eager, Nachum and Serkei Wimmer gladly continued to pay the dentist for Romek's internship. For about four years, Romek made bridges and crowns in addition to assisting with patients in the dental chair.

People were still trying to convince themselves that the newly brazen antisemitism they were witnessing was just a phase. Jews throughout history had seen and lived through uncomfortable times before. So people tried to do normal things, like going to their local dentist and attending synagogue, as much as possible.

Jabotinsky Trajectory
Beitar, Kraków, and Jerusalem

Romek also spent time with the Jewish youth group Beitar. Beitar was founded in Riga, Latvia, in the 1920s by Vladimir Jabotinsky, a Jewish nationalist who believed that Jews would continue to be picked on so long as Jews had no homeland of their own. Beitar was the name of the last Jewish fort to fall in the Bar Kochba revolt against Roman occupation of the Land of Israel in 138 C.E. Jabotinsky advocated for picking up where Bar Kochba left off, contending that if Jews could fend for themselves in their own land, they could fend for themselves anywhere. He advocated for Jews to learn self-defense and work toward the re-establishment of the Jewish homeland. Jabotinsky was reacting to both antisemitic sentiments in Latvia as well as current events in other countries, including British Mandate Palestine, where reports of attacks on Jews surfaced with frightening regularity. Arabs rioted in Hebron and the Galilee; throughout Europe, country after country passed laws to marginalize Jews.

Jabotinsky connected the dots to show that isolated violent incidents were not so isolated. Beitar popularized the idea that threats to Jews could only be addressed by recreating the ancient Jewish state of Israel. Beitar sought to instill a Zionist backbone among Jewish youth. By the mid-1930s, there were hundreds of Beitar chapters in Poland with thousands of Jewish youth. On one level, it was comforting to be among other Jews at a time when many non-Jewish neighbors were making life uncomfortable; on another level, Beitar offered blunt answers to the cold reality that would soon eclipse Europe's Jews. Life in Europe seemed bad for its Jews because it was.

And it was going to get worse unless Jews picked themselves up, left, and reestablished a Jewish state. Jabotinsky traveled across Europe speaking of a big, dark cloud that took little imagination to see because everyone felt it. Romek heard Jabotinsky speak in Kraków in 1938 on the cusp of World War II. "Polish Jews are living on the edge of a volcano!" Jabotinsky warned. "Catastrophe is approaching. I see a terrible picture… the volcano that will soon spew out its flames of extermination." Jabotinsky urged Jews to leave Europe lest the bubbling volcano erupt and engulf everyone.

Jabotinsky's oration impacted Romek deeply. While Romek had the heard doom-and-gloom routine before, Jabotinsky uniquely advocated for Europe's Jews to do something about it. He stressed that Jews should learn to defend themselves. He also advocated for Europe's Jews to join their brethren in the Jews' historical home and be prepared to fight for the Land of Israel, which was then governed by the British. Jabotinsky stressed that when a dynamic antisemite like Hitler says he wants to eradicate Jews from Europe, he should be taken seriously. Believe your enemy, Jabotinsky warned.

Unfortunately, many like Nachum Wimmer just saw Hitler as a relatively harmless rabble-rouser who would be put down eventually by calmer heads. After all, Nachum had fought for Austria in World War I; he was proud of his Austrian roots and knew that the army had a way of dealing with loudmouths. People knew him and his family to be good citizens.

While Romek Wimmer enjoyed Beitar, his father was not thrilled with his son's activities with the group. Self-defense? Talk of moving to the Holy Land? Why? The laws that had been passed were just a phase. Historically, Jews had lived through worse times. After all, Nachum had deep roots in Austria and Poland and believed that he and his fellow Jews were agile, resourceful, and rooted enough to weather any storm, including the present day. If it meant moving to another place in Poland, so be it.

The specific question of whether to stay or leave Wieliczka came to a head in the Wimmer household one night. With little business to speak of and savings rapidly ebbing away, Nachum Wimmer sought to move his family. It took him a few weeks to speak with the right people, but he secured a rare visa for himself to the United States, the *Goldena Medina* [Golden Land]. Though supposedly paved with golden opportunities, America had the reputation among the Orthodox folk as a "Treifa" Medina – a spiritually vacuous country where a people's distinctive religious culture would gradually, but inevitably, melt away.

Nachum planned to work as much as he could and send money back to secure visas for everyone. His wife, Serkei, who generally laid down the law in the Wimmer household, had other ideas. "No, we will not separate," she said. Perhaps she objected to the concept of separating the family in general; she may also have rejected the idea of going to America - where tales of Jews' losing their religion in and to the Land of Opportunity made it a *treif* [non-kosher] option. The Wimmers stayed together.

Author: Jabotinsky published his will and testament in 1935, inserting an unusual clause demanding that, should he perish outside the Land of Israel, his remains should be brought to Israel, but only by order of the future Jewish government that would come to power. As fate would have it, Jabotinsky died in New York in 1940. In the early years of the Jewish state, Israeli Prime Minister David Ben-Gurion refused to issue the order to exhume Jabotinsky's body, transport it across the Atlantic, and rebury him in Israel. Ben-Gurion was Jabotinsky's ideological rival in life and saw no reason to put those differences aside after Jabotinsky's death when subjected to intense lobbying by Jabotinsky's protege Menachem Begin. In 1964, Levi Eshkol succeeded Ben-Gurion as Israel's prime minister.

With an eye toward national reconciliation between the adherents of Ben Gurion and those of the Begin/Jabotinsky camp, Eshkol ordered that a state funeral be given for the reburial of Jabotinsky's remains in the military cemetery in West Jerusalem's Mount Herzl.

In 1964, Papa Romek and Nana Sala Wimmer – by then known as Jack and Sally Wimmer – visited Israel for the first time. Seeing and walking the land that their parents and grandparents had prayed for and dreamed of but never lived to see fortified their Jewish pride immeasurably. As they were walking through the streets of Jerusalem, they noticed a commotion. People were being moved off the streets onto sidewalks. Barricades suddenly divided the sidewalks from the street. They noticed a sudden increased police presence.

Romek asked a policeman: "Hey, Officer, what's going on here now?"

"Jabotinsky is being reburied in Israel today. We are setting up for the procession."

"Wow! What an amazing man he was; I saw him in Kraków, Poland, in 1935 in my Beitar days! I heard him and only wish that my parents would have listened to him."

Impressed that this American tourist knew of Jabotinsky, the policeman asked Romek a few questions, radioed a fellow officer, and told Romek to stay put. Within minutes, the policeman moved a barricade and whisked Romek to the front of the procession, where he was given the honor of carrying the coffin with several others.

Menachem Begin himself signed a certificate given to Romek to commemorate that "Chaim Avraham Wimmer (Romek's proper Hebrew name) served as an honored pall bearer as *Yisrael Zev Jabotinsky Shav La Moledet*. ["Yisrael Zev Jabotinsky returns to the Homeland" for reinterment]. Romek framed and proudly displayed this certificate in his home for all to see.

To Romek, it signified his place in modern Jewish history; it testified that Jabotinsky understood two ideas that Romek's parents did not. First, Jews should never hesitate to believe their enemies; and second, nothing can fortify Jewish backbones worldwide better than a Jewish homeland in historical Israel. With a solemn nod toward a path not taken by his own family, Romek nonetheless saw himself as a proud witness to Jabotinsky's vision coming full circle.

Brave Mother and the First Holy 32

Romek vividly recalled when dark times turned even darker. On the day before Rosh Hashana 1939, the Germans came to Wieliczka with trucks and a few dozen barking soldiers. They had a list of prominent Jews to round up. When the Wimmers heard the commotion from the town square outside their home, they peeked out the window and realized what was happening. Nachum Wimmer ran to a crawl space near the roof to hide.

A German soldier pounded on the door. As he was about to ram it open, Serkei Wimmer opened it up. "Wimmer, *schnell*! Where is Herr Wimmer?" Rather than wait for an explanation, the soldier grabbed 16-year-old Romek and took him outside to the idling trucks.

"Stop!" pleaded Serkei. "He's just 16 and of no use to you! He's a child!"

The soldier looked at Romek, a young, scared lad, and then at Serkei. Her eyes were fierce and defiant, like a lioness protecting her cub. Miraculously, the German soldier relented to a mother's raw plea.

The other 32 people rounded up that day were not as fortunate. The trucks drove them to a forest in Taszyce, a few kilometers south of town where they were lined up and used as target practice for the bloodthirsty German soldiers. The Germans deliberately took these prominent men on the day before Rosh Hashana to send a message: "Don't even think of messing with us. You and your rituals cannot save you. Germany is in charge now. You, your leaders, and your God are meaningless."

A Polish peasant who witnessed the massacre ran to Wieliczka and told everyone. Instead of preparing for the High Holy Days, the remaining Jews of Wieliczka buried and mourned their 32 innocent brethren.

Among the 32 were three of Romek's uncles: *Fetter* [Uncle] Moishe Wimmer, Fetter Yankel Wimmer, and Fetter Berel Vishinsky. Romek knew most of the other 32, too: a shoemaker who was renting an apartment from the Wimmers and lived across the hall named Moishe Fischer, along with others who davened at Congregation Dorshei Tov, the shul down the block from the Wimmers' home.

The shock of the Germans' first stab at Wieliczka's Jews stayed with Romek; he said Kaddish for the 32 on the anniversary of their murders each year of his life to remember theirs. Unfortunately, more shocking cruelty would soon follow.

Scarcity Forces Togetherness

In occupied Poland, the Germans deemed it important to keep males – young males in particular – busy with manual labor. It was an efficient way to keep the populace in check with the added bonus of exploiting free labor. At this point, the Jews who had stayed in Wieliczka had nowhere to go even if they wanted to. No place was particularly safe for Jews at this point. The Germans required the Jews to report to the town square daily for work assignments – some were sent to clean streets, shovel snow, and build things. Not all of the manual labor assigned had a real purpose other than to keep people occupied. If people were working, they were not plotting to organize resistance.

For the next three years, the Wimmers' life in Wieliczka became increasingly unbearable. Commerce was scarce. People had no bread. There were bread lines – not only for Jews, but Poles, too. If a Pole saw a Jew at or near the front of the bread line, they would usually force the Jew out of line, just like Sala had experienced in Dąbrowa Górnicza.

Kraków had a ghetto for Jews at this point; many of the city's Jews fled to their brethren in Wieliczka to avoid it. Every Jewish family took in other Jewish families, and crowding grew severe. New decrees were issued frequently. Jews had to wear armbands, then yellow Jewish stars on their clothing. Then they could not walk on the street. No one attended school. If Jews were not at a work location assigned by the Germans, they were expected to remain at home.

In the early years of the war, the Wimmers, the Szlases, and the Drexlers all witnessed flashes of haphazard German extermination and terror: pogroms, executions, and individual or group murders coupled with laws passed to deprive and dehumanize. Deprivation of civic rights, exclusion from all sources of livelihood, seclusion in ghettos, hunger, and disease took a heavy toll on the Jewish population. But it was messy and inefficient. The Nazis' compulsory labor policies helped the German war effort but also lacked the elegance and efficiency of a well-oiled German operation.

In late 1941, the Germans decided to approach the "Jewish Problem" systematically to wipe out all of Europe's 11 million Jews. Instead of confining Jews to ghettos or small towns where Jews were easy targets for forced labor, the Germans established the first death camps and more work camps in 1942. These were all deemed "cleansing" activities – a sanitized name for the complete extermination of the Jews.

Despite the barrage of haphazard edicts, the forced menial labor, and scarce food, the fact that everyone came home in the evening gave the Wimmer family some solace. That changed on August 26, 1942, the day the Germans decided to make Wieliczka *Judenrein* as part of Aktzion Reinhard – the concerted German effort to rid Poland of its Jews.

Judenrein in Wieliczka, August 26, 1942

The Judenrein order was not a complete surprise. With living conditions deteriorating as the war progressed, Romek's brother, Henyek (Chanan Tzvi), had predicted that life was about to get much worse about a week before the order. Henyek had a work assignment in Plaszów. That's where the notorious Nazi Amon Goeth (of Schindler's List fame) had just been appointed commandant and began to gleefully terrorize the petrified forced laborers.

When Henyek came home one night, he told the family that the Germans had started randomly shooting people while they were working. Random, as in, for no reason at all. The shootings instilled a fear that did not make sense. At least people could understand the point of slave labor. But here, people were working as quickly as possible to further the German war effort (albeit against their will) and all of a sudden – bang! The fright kept people in line, and those who appeared unable to handle these working conditions were sent to a death camp called Belzec. The Wimmers could hardly process this gruesome information.

Through it all, Henyek had to report back to work daily. Henyek asked his parents if he could take a pillow from home to the Plaszów work camp. He had heard there would soon be changes and he did not know when he would be able to return home again. Life was extremely tense with random rules squeezing them ever further from the life they once lived. Even so, the Wimmers gave no second thought about sending a pillow with their teenage child to the work camp. The next day, Henyek reported to camp with this small item of comfort from a home to which he would not return. They never found out what happened to Henyek.

A few days later, on August 26, 1942, the Germans ordered all of Wieliczka's Jews to an *Umschlagplatz*, a large common area near a train station closeby. You could bring no more than a small bag. Just as Henyek had foretold, life was about to change forever.

At the Umschlagplatz, Jews were forced into a line, with each person taking their turn for a grim evaluation by the German officers seated at a table in front of the line. Nachum, Serkei, Romek, and Romek's youngest two siblings, Shlomo and Sabina, huddled together in line hoping and praying they would not be separated.

That was not to be. As the Wimmers came to the front of the line, one German pointed to Romek. "You! Right!" he barked. As Romek was being whisked toward the group of other able-bodied, mostly young men on the right, he saw the officer point the rest of his family leftward. Romek made eye contact with his father and started to bolt left. Nachum's eyes, though pained, were steeled – clearly intended to give his son encouragement and confidence to overcome whatever may come next. The first thing that came was a flurry of wooden batons that stopped Romek in his determined tracks and forced him back.

Nineteen-year-old Romek and everyone else forced to the right were taken to a nearby school where they stayed overnight. The Wimmer family, minus their two older sons, were shoved into cattle cars and taken by train to Belzec.

German SS and police personnel at Belzec swiftly moved along the Jews who were arriving from all over Poland. First, the Jews handed over all valuables in their possession – the bags they were allowed to take with them to the Umschlagplatz and whatever valuable clothing they may have been wearing. Then, they forced the Jews to undress and run through the "tube" – a waiting area that led directly into gas chambers that were cruelly and deceptively labeled as "showers." The guards sealed the chamber doors and started pumping in carbon monoxide. Prisoners removed the dead, and the death factory started preparing for the next set of trains to arrive.

Surviving Slave Labor

Not all the Jews of Wieliczka went to the Umschlagplatz. Some parents had encouraged their children to hide; some who were ill simply stayed home that day. The Nazis suspected that some had remained back. The SS went from house to house, grabbing whatever they wanted, found those who had stayed behind, and shot them on the spot.

On orders, Romek and the others who had been taken to the school spent the next three days burying the dead. Romek recognized many of his family's friends and neighbors among the dead, including those from his synagogue. Taking the bodies through ransacked homes for burial was a gruesome task. However, these victims' defiance in not going to the Umschlagplatz at least afforded them the dignity of a burial by their brethren, which was rare for Jews in late 1942 Poland. As Romek buried friends and neighbors during the three days after he separated from his family at the Umschlagplatz, he did not know that his worst nightmare would also come to fruition. Very few, if any, survived the Belzec death machine; Romek did not know that he had become an orphan.

After three days of burying the dead and cleaning streets under SS orders, Romek and the others were again selected and divided. Some were sent to Plaszów, the munitions factory where Henyek had been taken, and others to Rozwadów.

Romek came to Rozwadów with others he knew from Wieliczka. Most were in their late teens and twenties; some were older but deemed hardy enough to work. All had lost family. At 6 a.m., the camp was woken and everyone had to line up to be counted. The Germans obsessed over counting the prisoners, doing so frequently. Next was the bread line; everyone stood in line for a small piece of bread and a small cup of coffee. That was the day's ration.

He had a few friends with him, including his shul's spiritual leader, Rabbi Pinchus Leibush Frankel, who was assigned to work with him in the steel mill called Stalowa Wola. Their job was to unload raw iron. The raw material was heavy and handling it made people ill at times. The Nazis divided the slave labor into subgroups of eight or ten to unload individual train cars filled with material.

Romek and his friend Shlemek (Sam) Poznanski saw that some of their co-workers could not handle the hard work and developed a rotation of sorts to take turns unloading when they were not being supervised directly by Germans; the Poles that had been left in charge didn't care how the work got done as long as it did. One time, when there was a Polish holiday and the Germans and Poles had left the Jewish slave labor unsupervised, Romek and Poznanski commandeered a crane that was on site. The crane had a magnet. Though Romek had never used a crane in his life, he figured out how to lower the magnet, pick up the steel, and move it. A rare easy day that propped up morale that day ever so slightly.

With melted steel, the prisoners made cannons and other munitions. While the melted steel was still red hot, 12 people removed the newly formed item from the frame. After it cooled, they hammered out the imperfections. Hard, grueling work. Some Poles were also forced to work in the steel mill, though they were treated slightly better. Romek often sneaked into the area where the Poles worked to grab a pot of hot tea to share with his group. Romek ignored the personal risk of leaving his post, and his friends worked quicker to cover for him in his absence.

What will they do to me? Kill me? They'd be down a worker; if they want us to work, we need some nourishment, thought Romek. They were given a small piece of bread and some water that did not adequately nourish people for the hard work they were doing. Within ten weeks of coming to the steel mill with 1,200 people, only 320 remained. Romek's teapot helped him and those around him increase their odds of survival.

Because the Germans needed the steel mill to produce, they had an infirmary for people who needed care to recuperate and get back to work. When he was not working at the mill, Romek worked for Dr. Goldstein, who ran the infirmary. Everyone was tired. Extremely tired. Some were sicker than others, but everyone was worn down from the hard work and meager rations. Romek helped the doctor document everything as required. They couldn't simply excuse people from work for being tired, so Romek and the doctor rotated people in and out of the infirmary. Sometimes, they would dip a thermometer in hot water so they could document a fever. That would enable their exhausted coworker to stay in the infirmary another day.

How did Romek stay healthy? "I don't know," he said. "God's will, I managed." He explained how he slept in the kitchen on a bench next to the oven. A Jewish person who ran the kitchen sometimes would need something from the infirmary. Romek bartered for the relatively cozy spot on the bench for pulling occasional favors. Of course, he had to run back to the barracks in the morning before wake-up time, but he preferred having to wake up early and risking being seen oversleeping in the barracks with hungry bedbugs. Romek remained an early riser for the rest of his life. The benefits of getting up before others allowed him to accomplish much in the wee morning hours, often more than many do in a day.

Yom Kippurim

Yom Kippur of 1941 played an oversized role in Shaya's life as Yom Kippur of 1942 did in Romek's life. As the horrors of the Holocaust were unfolding throughout Europe and especially Poland, that single day – that holy day of Yom Kippur – stood out above all others for both of them. What they witnessed and went through on that day shook them to their core. The events on Yom Kippur in different areas of Poland – Romek in the Rozwadów work camp in 1942, Shaya in a forced farewell at home in Lopianka in 1941 – stirred them from sleep as they often re lived the momentous shock and tension even decades later. Nonetheless, they each girded themselves daily to move beyond those times and focus on the day at hand as they worked to secure their respective futures and legacies.

Post-Yom Kippur 1941
A Parting of Ways

At the time, Shaya and his family were living in the small Polish village of Łopianka. They had moved a few times since the war broke out, hoping to move just far enough from the battlefront to avoid it while staying close enough to hopefully move back when things returned to normal. Unfortunately, the situation progressed from bad to worse and never returned to normal. Łopianka was a few train stations away from the Treblinka death camp. Just before the High Holy days of 1941, a young Jewish man who had escaped the Warsaw Ghetto came to Łopianka and described how he had jumped from a cattle car on its way to Treblinka the prior evening. He threw his coat first as a decoy, waited for a few shots, and jumped as the guard on duty was reloading. After narrowly escaping death, the jumper was shocked to find other Jews still living relatively normally in Shaya's village.

The man described how the Jews of Warsaw were herded into the cattle cars, dying for a drink of water. Jumping from a moving train was the best alternative. The Jews of Łopianka were delusional if they thought they were insulated from the horror that had enveloped Warsaw's Jews, the man said. It was a matter of time. And there wasn't much left.

What choice was there at this point? Tragedy loomed. It was in the air. The Treblinka train jumper opened eyes to the foreboding stark reality. As Yom Kippur approached without any specific threat on the horizon, the Jews in Łopianka threw themselves into prayer. Jacob Schloss, a trained chazzan, led a small gathering of Jews praying together for (what they did not know at the time would be) the last time. Years later, Shaya spoke lovingly of his father leading the Yom Kippur prayer services that year in a small home with approximately 20 people. "You could hear a pin drop," Shaya said. He would often return to that scene in his mind. He would close his eyes and recite some of the liturgy by heart along with his father until he would eventually taper off and then sigh as if disgusted with his own voice, saying something like, "You should have heard my dear father, a beautiful voice, not like mine." He would usually add, "That was the last time I heard my father singing." Of those who gathered to hear Jacob Schloss on that Yom Kippur day in Łopianka in 1941, only Shaya and one other person survived the war.

Praying to be inscribed in the Book of Life when the Nazis were closing in to efficiently fill the Book of Death with new names assuredly was on everyone's mind. "Who will live and who will die?" – a part of the Yom Kippur liturgy – was unfortunately answered all too quickly that year. Immediately after Yom Kippur, the Jewish leaders were informed that the Jews of the town would be brought to Treblinka within the next day or so, just as the train jumper had warned.

"If anyone has a way of helping themselves, they should do so," warned the president of the *Judenrat* [Jewish Council] of the Łopianka ghetto. While those in the ghetto all had heard of the trains to the camps, they had managed by the grace of God to that point to avoid it. The general sense of foreboding that had been festering for many months was now immediate and urgent. The stark news from the Judenrat's president burst the bubble of hope of their lives ever returning to normal.

Families huddled together deciding what, if anything, should be done. Plead for mercy? Stick together at all costs? Run? Hide? Fight? Shaya's family felt paralyzed and cried on each other's shoulders. His mother, Miriam, girded herself and made the decision.

When the biblical Jacob was to meet his brother, Esau, after years on the run, Jacob feared the confrontation. It was not long before that Esau had wanted to kill him; now he heard that Esau was traveling with a pack of 400 soldiers. Jacob's next three moves served as a template for generations of diaspora Jews in unfriendly environs –

prayer, appeasement, and dividing the camp. Immediately after Yom Kippur, Miriam felt that all possible prayers had been said. Her husband Jacob's heartfelt, melodious davening had left no dry eyes among the worshippers earlier that day.

Appeasing the Germans was not an option – anything of material value had been taken by then and, as the train jumper confirmed, the Germans were out for blood. Remembering biblical Jacob's tactic of dividing the camp so that if some were attacked, others might survive, Miriam pleaded with Shaya and his younger teenage sister Klara (his older brother and older sister were out of the house by then), "Run! Run away and hide in the forest."

"Fight!" she continued. "Your father and I are not well enough to run anymore, but you, dear children, must do whatever you can to survive!" Implicit in her pleas was a prayer, a bargain with God of sorts – if we put our faith in your hands, God, and do our part to divide the camp as the biblical Jacob did, may God bless the children of me and my Jacob with the fortitude and fortune to survive this terrible time.

At first, Shaya still felt paralyzed. "Leave my parents and my little sister, how could I?" he asked.

Klara mustered words first. Like the biblical Ruth said to her older mother-in-law Naomi: "Where you go, I will go; I'm not leaving you." She resolutely refused to leave her parents.

As if on cue, two of Shaya's friends, Chuzik and Jelen, came running in with timely information. Their families had made some sort of deal with a local Polish farmer for them. The farmer agreed to hide the two young men and had room for a third.

"You want to come with us?" they asked Shaya.

Before Shaya could give it a second thought or have a chance to say no, his parents and sister started hugging and kissing him goodbye. This was an opportunity to act immediately on his mother's words;

his parents likely saw this as a message from God Himself to run away. "Run! Run to the forest and survive!" Those words stuck with Shaya throughout his life. He did not want to leave the house without his parents and sister first promising him that they would leave Łopianka and run to hide in the dense forest nearby.

Through all the pain and fear that would soon come, Shaya relied heavily on his mother's prayer at the darkest of times as his inner rallying cry. From that point on, he was perpetually in survival mode.

Yom Kippur 1942
Murder of a Rabbi

In Rozwadów, Romek Wimmer was among the 100 workers forced to go to work in the Stalowa Wola steel mill. The day started with a small bit of food, some black coffee, and a few-mile march to the mill.

Romek's group from Wieliczka had somehow stayed together through several selection points. The group looked out for each other; despite the weariness, pulling for each other allowed them to lean against one another, giving the group a collective strength that none could have mustered on their own. Though indistinguishable in appearance at that point, Rabbi Pinchus Leibush Frenkel's presence also gave the group a measure of comfort. Rabbi Frenkel, a second-generation rabbi of the town of Wieliczka, knew Romek and the Wimmer family well.

On Yom Kippur, while fasting, Rabbi Frenkel, Romek, and ten others from Wieliczka unloaded scrap metal from a trolley car, just as they had done in each of the previous days. In the middle of the day, the SS commandant of the camp, Josef Schwammberger, visited the workplace and singled out Romek's group for a quiet investigation. Schwammberger asked the group for a German-speaking prisoner to come forward. Romek and one other prisoner spoke German, and the two approached Schwammberger. He then asked for a list.

"Of what?" they asked.

"Write down the names of the men in this group. Give me this list tonight in Rozwadów when you come back from work here. Back to work, Jews."

With that odd request, Schwammberger left the prisoners to continue their hard, menial work unloading and loading scrap metal on the holiest day of the year.

Schwammberger was looking for the good Rabbi Frenkel, and Romek knew it. The commandant never had cared to know anyone's names before; apparently, someone trying to curry favor had tipped him off that there was a town's rabbinic leader in the group and the commandant saw an opportunity.

At the end of their shift, late at night after Yom Kippur had ended, the prisoners marched back to Rozwadów. Romek gave Rabbi Frenkel his ration of a half-rotten tomato because he knew the rabbi had been fasting all day. It was to be the last morsel of food for him.

The fellow German-speaking Jew, Jonas, the *Juden Älteste* [Jewish appointee] approached Romek and asked him for the list of people in Romek's group. Romek refused.

"I will not give the list," Romek replied defiantly." What will they do to me? They already took my parents, my family. I am not afraid of what will happen to me if I don't provide a list of names."

Romek understood that handing over a list with Rabbi Frenkel's name would put the revered rabbi directly in the SS man's cross hairs. Even at his own personal risk, Romek wanted no part of it. Others in the group were aghast as Romek refused to write anything down or help the kapo draft a list.

Romek repeated: "I will not write down names of these fellows. I will not give a list to make anything easy. My parents were taken, my brothers, and my sister. What can they do to me that would make things worse for me?" he asked his fellow-prisoners again in rhetorical defiance.

Schwammberger then stormed in and demanded that everyone in Romek's group line up in front of all the others in Rozwadów. After everyone quickly fell into place, Schwammberger barked, "Frenkel, step forward!" David Frenkel, a cousin of the rabbi, one other relative named Frenkel, and Rabbi Frenkel all stepped out. "Not all of you! Only *Rabina* [Rabbi] Frenkel – you step forward!" As the others fell back into line, Rabbi Frenkel faced the growling Nazi. Romek stood in still horror only a few feet away. Schwammberger declared in German that the rabbi (blessed be his memory) had sabotaged the work and the German war effort that day.

"How? I was working with everyone else?!" Rabbi Frenkel pleaded.

"By fasting and making the other inmates fast, you made everyone weaker and slowed down the work. You are sentenced to death for this deliberate subterfuge."

With an additional layer of cruelty, the SS monster tauntingly asked the rabbi: "Who is more powerful: your God or my gun?"

His words were then translated into Polish to make sure everyone understood the sick power play at hand, though everyone fully understood.

Rabbi Frenkel pleaded again. "But I was working alongside the others! I was with them and we were all working!"

In mid-sentence, in the presence of dozens of his congregants-turned slave laborers, Schwammberger shot Rabbi Frenkel dead at close range.

The blood-soaked soil trembled as all of those present witnessed the murder in shocked silence. Proud of himself, Schwammberger put his gun securely back in his holster and ordered two prisoners to haul Rabbi Frenkel's body away in a wheelbarrow. A holy, innocent man, a third-generation rabbi, murdered in front of his flock immediately after Yom Kippur and taken out like bulk trash.

Romek stood less than five feet away from the atrocity as it happened. Though powerless to stop it, Romek often replayed the entire scene of Rabbi Frenkel's heinous murder and Schwammberger's casual smugness and self-satisfaction with the Rabbi's murder in his mind.

Author: Papa Wimmer often recounted that even though he had lost his entire family and there were plenty of horrific events that could cause nightmares, this post-Yom Kippur murder was the one thing that interrupted his sleep on some nights. I remember sleeping over at Nana and Papa's and hearing Papa's scream and Nana calming him down. Memories like that do not fade easily. However, unlike with all other terrors and indignities Papa suffered and witnessed during those years, Papa's long memory helped him avenge Rabbi Frenkel's murder directly decades later...

On the Run

After Shaya left his family, he and his friends met up with the manager of a farm, who told them which barn to sleep in. It was about a mile away. When the three made it to the barn, they lay down in the hay but could not sleep. They talked throughout the night brainstorming how they would get through this ordeal. Shortly after sunrise, they peeked through small holes in the barn as they saw the German gendarmes going from house to house pulling people out. Old people and children were put in wagons. Those who could walk well enough were lined up like soldiers and marched to a nearby train station. The scene described by the young train jumper from the Warsaw Ghetto was now playing out before them in Łopianka. The SS officers' methodical roundup of Jews worked with franchise-like uniformity. The German death machine rolled through Poland, in cities and towns big and small like Warsaw, Łopianka, and Wieliczka with alarming speed and consistency.

As the procession of the forced marchers was passing the farm where Shaya and his friends were hiding, the manager of the farm burst into the barn screaming: "Jelen! Szlas! Chuzik! Come out from where you are hiding; I have to talk to you!" This did not sound promising; they ignored him at first. As he started to yell louder, they feared he would attract attention and came out. "You must leave this barn immediately: go join your families."

The barn was about 100 meters from the main road. They immediately ran in the opposite direction into a huge apple orchard and lost each other. Shaya ran and ran and ran – just as his mother had told him. By midday, Shaya found a hole in the ground, covered himself with grass, and lay there until sundown. Miraculously, Shaya and his friends found each other after dark. They decided that running on their own was too hard. Chuzik's family had a designated meet-up location. That was their first stop the next morning, and Chuzik reunited with his family.

Shaya and Jelen found a group of families who had run to the forests from Łopianka. Among them was Jelen's family. The group had paid a friendly Polish farmer to bring them food and news from outside the forest. Shaya approached him. "You know my father, Jacob Szlas, right?"

"Sure, the grocer."

"Yes. Did my family leave Łopianka before the roundup?"

"Yes, they ran to the forest."

Shaya's mind and heart raced as soon as he heard those words.

"But the German police caught them and a few others and sent them on the next train to Treblinka."

As if that news weren't horrible enough, the Polish farmer gave the group more bad news to digest: "I heard that the Germans know about Jews hiding all around the forest; I can't do anything for you anymore. They will likely be coming within the next 24 hours to round up whoever had evaded them."

Alone But Inspired

Shaya felt like giving up after the farmer's double whammy of bad news. His friends had found their families and his family was gone. Shaya was the only person on his own in the group. Suddenly alone in a cruel world, he could barely process the bevy of emotions that swirled around him – exhaustion, fear, grief, pain, sadness. Seeing his friends conferring with their families gave him an idea – dig deep within and conjure up what his dear parents might want him to do. The blueprint was short but clear. Shaya replayed the scene of saying goodbye to his parents and sister. His mother's parting defiant prayer words were seared in his head. "Run and you will survive!" Those words, "Run and you will survive," girded him to steel himself throughout whatever would next come his way.

The group was too large and could not stay together. Strength was not in numbers with the Germans expected within hours. Shaya needed a plan. He keenly observed the families in the forest huddle among themselves as they each strategized their next moves. One woman left a group and came back soon thereafter. She whispered something to her husband and three sons as they all nodded quietly to each other. Clearly, they had secured a viable place to hide. Minutes later, they slipped away.

Shaya followed. They began to run as they realized they were being followed. But Shaya kept on running, too. They begged him to stop. "Yes, we paid a farmer who will hide us, but the farmer is only expecting us five," they said. "If he sees another person, he may ask for more money, which we do not have, or worse, not allow any of us on his farm." He understood and agreed to leave if the farmer put up any fuss about an extra person. Thankfully, the farmer didn't care. So Shaya stayed with the family for two days until he came up with another plan.

Stasik

The family who reluctantly let Shaya follow them from the forest to the farm unfortunately did not survive. Later he learned that the farmer who hid them eventually turned them in. Shaya only stayed with them for a few days. As he left, he apologized for any trouble he may have caused, thanked them, and wished them well.

As he left the barn, he grabbed a rake and began walking. After walking past miles of trees, farms, and ranches in the Polish countryside, he was famished. He decided to assume a new role and character. Rake in hand, he found a farmhouse and knocked on the front door. "Blessed is Jesus," he said as a Polish farm girl opened the door. She let him in and gave him food and drink, and he went on his way.

"The Poles were big religious fanatics in those days; that's how they greeted each other," he later explained.

Shaya repeated the act more than a few times. He came across an old man loading a horse-drawn wagon with sacks of potatoes. "Blessed is Jesus," they said to each other.

"Where are you from? How did you get here?" the man asked.

Shaya introduced himself as Stasik, a common Polish name, and explained that his town near the German border was overrun by the Germans and that anyone who could run away did. He was simply looking for work. "Can I help you load?" he asked.

"Sure," the old man replied.

They loaded the wagon full of potatoes until dusk and rode back to the man's farm after dark. After they unloaded the wagon, the farmer introduced his wife, and the three ate dinner. The elderly couple believed Shaya's story and did not sense he was a Jew from a few towns away. The farmer explained that he was behind on his seasonal work and asked "Stasik" to help him.

Shaya readily accepted and helped the farmer over the next few weeks. The couple's son, Peter, came to visit one day to check in on his parents and to offer his own help. Peter was shocked at how orderly things were at his parents' place. "Stasik," the farmer explained, "has been such a good worker." Peter was so impressed that he asked his parents if he could bring Stasik to his farm for a bit to help there. With things in order for the season, the older farmer acquiesced, and Shaya went off with Peter. At Peter's farm, Shaya helped with chores and was settling into a routine. He felt that he had found a home of sorts.

While he was chopping firewood outside one day, however, a man whom Shaya recognized approached the farm. Shaya nervously went about his business, trying not to blow his cover.

The man walked up to him with a Cheshire cat-like grin and simply asked: "Where's Peter?"

"Inside the house," he answered quietly, knowing full well that the person recognized him but hoping to be mistaken. Should he run? That would surely give it away. Stay put and hope for the best.

About a half hour later, Peter and the man came outside. They looked at "Stasik" as if to verify something. The man stared at Shaya and then nodded to Peter as if to say, "Yup, that's him." The man knew Shaya because they attended the same class in public school for several years. Shaya never forgot faces and, apparently, neither did this man.

The man shook Peter's hand and left. Noticeably shell-shocked, Peter hesitantly approached Shaya. But before Peter could say anything, Shaya came clean. "So now you know about me."

"Yes. You cannot stay here anymore. I am sorry, but you have to leave immediately." For Peter, the risk of a Pole being found hiding a Jew outweighed the many benefits "Stasik" provided him and his parents. That Shaya had helped this man at his farm and his parents' farm for months, working for nothing other than room and board, meant little at this point. The Jew had to leave.

"Please, you have been so kind and I appreciate that," Shaya said. "You have seen the hard work I did for you and your parents. Please, just one more night so I can plan out my next steps." As if finding another farm to avoid getting killed was some elaborate plan.

"Okay," Peter said. "You should know that your story is believable. I couldn't believe that you're a Jew. You certainly had me and my family fooled. Stick with it. You have a good chance you'll survive."

With that abrupt goodbye, he bought himself one more day to think about where he would run next. As he walked through fields and forests with no particular place to go, his mind raced. He knew that his parents and younger sister had been killed. He held out hope that his brother Isaac and sister Paja were still alive. Isaac had been drafted into the Russian army, so finding him would have to wait for the end of the war. Paja, however, was living in a small town in northern Poland when he last parted ways with her.

Shaya Planning with Paja

Shaya tried to find Paja by retracing his family's steps. His family had left Kowalówka in August 1941 when things started to turn for the worse. He had few good memories from Kowalówka, but at least he knew the area well. Shaya nervously knocked on the door at the Dembek family's farmhouse. The Dembeks had patronized Shaya's parents' store. "Mrs. Dembek was a good Polish woman; Mr. Dembek wasn't too good – the opposite of her," he later recalled.

Mrs. Dembek recognized him immediately, happily invited him in, and peppered him with questions. "Where have you been this whole year?" she asked. "Where are your parents and sister Klara? Hear anything about your brother Isaac?" Before he answered, Mrs. Dembek said, "I can give you regards from your sister Paja. She comes here about once a month and I give her some food. She's living in the ghetto in Ciechanowiec."

The spark of hope kindled by Mrs. Dembek's warm reception was tinged as Shaya noticed Mr. Dembek sitting, brooding, in a chair nearby, just listening. Mrs. Dembek continued the conversation as if her husband were not even there. She brought out some food and they ate together without Mr. Dembek saying a word. Shaya thanked them both and asked if he could sleep in their barn. Mrs. Dembek allowed it – again without consulting with Mr. Dembek.

On Sunday morning, Mrs. Dembek was working in the kitchen preparing food for the main Sunday meal. She served breakfast for herself and Shaya and continued the conversation, asking Shaya all about his previous year. In the late morning, Mr. Dembek came home from church looking irate. He then blurted out, "There are leaflets hanging all over the village which read: *Any person found to be feeding or hiding a Jew is liable for the death penalty!*"

He continued: "Germans liquidated all nearby ghettos and killed all the Jews." He looked at his wife indignantly with a "Do you really want to associate with that?" type of scowl. He then raised his voice and finally verbalized his clear displeasure with his wife's hospitality. Mr. Dembek had enough of indulging his wife. "Shaya, you cannot stay here. Leave immediately!"

The Dembeks looked and gestured at each other angrily as if they'd had this argument many times and did not need to express their respective sentiments in words. Shaya just sat there speechless, feeling sorry that he was the cause of their marital strife. But with no place to go, seeing how this drama would play out was his best option.

Mr. Dembek stormed out of the room and slammed the door as he left the house. Shaya pleaded with the sympathetic Mrs. Dembek, "Please, can I stay for a few days until things cool down a little?"

Mrs. Dembek agreed, but said, as if it wasn't already obvious, "We cannot let my husband know any of this. I'll show you where to go to hide in the barn and I will bring you some food when I can."

He hid in the barn and realized this was only a temporary solution. As sympathetic as Mrs. Dembek was, Mr. Dembek would catch on eventually and readily turn him in or become violent. He hoped for Mrs. Dembek's sake that Mr. Dembek would not get violent with her.

Keeping his mother's imploring words, "Keep running and you will survive," in mind, he resolved to do just that.

After two days in the Dembeks' barn, Mrs. Dembek opened the barn door and loudly and urgently called out in broad daylight: "Shaya, Shaya! Come out!"

Was she giving him up? His mind raced, but Mrs. Dembek softened her tone as she persisted. "Shaya, come out already!"

As he peeked out, he saw a familiar figure standing next to Mrs. Dembek. Shaya ran to his sister Paja and they hugged each other tightly and cried. For several minutes, they had no words, just tears. Mrs. Dembek cried with them, too, and then left them alone.

Shaya told Paja everything – about their parents and sister and their mother's words. There was more crying, this time even longer. He told of his run through the forest, his stay with the Polish farmer until his classmate had found him, and his educated guess to knock on the Dembeks' door. Now they both needed a plan as Mr. Dembek said that Germans had liquidated all remaining Jewish ghettos and were actively looking for Poles harboring Jews.

"Mr. Dembek is lying," said Paja. "He just wants us out of his hair. There are a few ghettos left, including in Ciechanowiec and some surrounding towns. While it may be a matter of time before the Germans get there, there are no such flyers that say that Poles harboring Jews will be killed. Most Poles are not like Mrs. Dembek anyway and don't need much encouragement to give up Jews in order to find some favor with the Germans."

"We still need a plan," Shaya said. He wanted to go to Ciechanowiec. Some of the people who fled Łopianka when he did were surely there. The last year had taught Shaya to be extremely self-reliant. A highly useful attribute, for sure, but joining up with people who have lasted this long and would also have your back during wartime would be optimal, Shaya thought. Paja wanted to stay with Mrs. Dembek for at least a few days. They decided to part ways temporarily; Shaya would check out Ciechanowiec to look for familiar people to plan next steps with. If he did not return within three days to Kowalówka, Paja would meet him in Ciechanowiec.

Aktzion!

Kowalówka was about 35 kilometers from Ciechanowiec. En route, Shaya encountered other random Jews scouring for food. "*Amcha?*" one man asked Shaya. *Amcha* means "your nation" – Jews would use it as a code word to identify one another. If the person hearing it didn't recognize the word, it might as well have been an innocuous cough or sneeze that would not easily give someone away as Jewish.

"Amcha," Shaya responded. The man was a forced day laborer who lived in the ghetto of Czyżew (about halfway between Kowalówka and Ciechanowiec). Shaya told him his story and that he'd been on the run since the Germans liquidated Łopianka. There had been an action in Czyżew when the war broke out, but since then, those who remained worked in various German industries during the day and went back to the ghetto in the evening.

"Don't get too comfortable," Shaya warned.

"But they need us," said the man. "We're doing indispensable work."

Shaya decided to assess the situation in Czyżew en route to Ciechanowiec and went back with the man. When they arrived, a Jewish guard was watching the front gate, so they had no problem getting in. Once inside the ghetto, they saw small groups of people congregating in the street. In one group, Shaya recognized a young man a few years older than he from Łopianka. He had run from Łopianka to Czyżew at the same time Shaya first escaped into the forest. Shaya entered what was apparently the middle of a conversation discussing current events, and in particular, what those events meant for the Jews. They knew about the camps and nearby Treblinka but believed the worst was behind them. "All of us here were already picked by the Nazis to work," explained Shaya's Lopianka friend, echoing Shaya's travel partner from earlier that evening.

The hour became late and Shaya needed a place to stay. The group told him to knock on the door of the ghetto's president. Shaya excused himself and found the president's house, noticing some commotion inside as he approached. He peered inside the window before knocking and saw everyone inside packing bundles and huddling together, apparently strategizing with urgency.

Shaya went back to the group and then understood the beginning part of the conversation he had missed. There was a rumor that the Germans were planning to liquidate the ghetto soon. The president believed it. Shaya believed it. The group in the street apparently did not. "Please, we all have to believe this and make plans for how we can all get through this," Shaya implored. "Why do you think Czyżew is safe? You survived one action, that's great, but the Germans are out for blood!" As much as Shaya wanted to cultivate some peers to rely on, these people were deluding themselves about their "indispensability" to the Germans.

Mid-conversation, Shaya heard the sound of rumbling horses from outside the ghetto gate. The group either pretended they didn't hear it or perhaps just wished they hadn't as they continued to discuss the matter, paralyzed by their wishful delusion. Shaya needed no prompting, though; he had seen this play out before. Exasperated with the group, he quietly rushed toward the ghetto wires to examine the situation. In the dark night, he saw a silhouette of a soldier smoking a cigarette on the other side of the ghetto wire. Another soldier called out to him, "*Schlofen, schlofen!*" beckoning the smoker to go to sleep already.

"Oh God, why did the rumor have to be right?" Shaya asked himself.

The Germans had indeed surrounded the ghetto. Shaya bolted toward the ghetto's back fence, where he found an open sewer, crawled under the ghetto wires, and slowly made his way through the muck. When he was able to run, Shaya came across a slew of obstacles in the dark – bushes, discarded wires, large branches from broken trees. He must have made some noise, as the next thing he heard was machine-gun fire in his direction. Shaya crawled on his stomach as fast as he could. When the gunfire died down, Shaya decided he was far enough from Czyżew to start running again. His mother's words barely echoed in his head: Shaya's urge to run to safety kicked in instinctively by now.

He didn't know where he was running to, but he kept running and falling, getting cut by wires, tearing clothing, slicing up his body. Shaya struggled like this for more than an hour and reached a canal. Other fleeing Jews were also there but seemed afraid to talk to Shaya or each other. Desperate and confused, everybody he saw ran chaotically in different directions. Not knowing how to swim, Shaya stood by the canal for a few minutes, hesitating about what to do. Again, the instinct to run kicked into gear as Shaya realized the danger of staying too close to a ghetto being liquidated. He jumped in the thankfully not-too-deep water and waded through it.

Once on the other side of the canal, Shaya felt somewhat safer. Within the last 12 hours, he had left the relative security of Mrs. Dembek's barn, took what he thought would be a small detour to Czyżew while en route to Ciechanowiec, tried to strategize with other Jews, heard Nazis waiting in ambush, crawled through a sewer, dodged bullets, ran through obstacles in the dark and crossed unknown waters, landing himself drenched and bruised into a forest on a cool day pre-dawn in November 1942. To feel warmer, Shaya tried walking quickly. He walked for hours through the forest – alone, wet, cold, hungry, and tired. Shaya collapsed under some trees when he could no longer stand and slept until sunrise.

At daybreak, he saw some farmhouses in the distance and decided to find out where his nightmarish run had landed him. Shaya approached the nearest farm and met a farmer starting his day. Aghast, but apparently sympathetic at Shaya's appearance, the older farmer started questioning Shaya before he even said a word. "Who are you? Where are you going? What happened to you?"

Shaya blurted out everything he had experienced within the last 24 hours. Stunned, the farmer offered some bread and milk and told Shaya what town he was in and the nearby villages. Shaya thanked him and headed toward Kowalówka to try to meet up and strategize with Paja. Paja was not there, however. Sensing danger in Kowalówka, Mrs. Dembek packed up Paja with some food and Paja headed to Ciechanowiec hoping to meet Shaya there before he came back for her.

Finding Good Poles

Miraculously, Paja and Shaya chose the same back road and unknowingly headed toward each other. Paja's tears began to flow as she saw the blood stains, bruises, and scratches over Shaya's face and hands along with his torn and dirty clothing. The sight of her little brother looking like a battlefield refugee compounded the months of ghetto living. It was as if Shaya's hellish appearance summarized their lives at this point. And she could not get out a word. Only tears and hysterical sobs. Shaya made her sit down on a big rock and tried calming her down. When the bawling gave way to periodic muffled sobs, Shaya told Paja everything he had just experienced. When he finished, she finally composed herself and said, "You must be very hungry. Please take some bread and butter from my bag."

"I can't eat right now. We have to figure out where to go next."

Shaya's survival instinct was already well-trained to come before satisfying any hunger pangs.

"Remember the Schwartzes?" asked Paja.

Mrs. Schwartz was a regular customer at their parents' grocery. She had a sick husband and three small children to feed. Their parents didn't even bother keeping a tab for her; she needed help and they gave it readily. Perhaps their parents' merit would help them find some refuge with Mrs. Schwartz, now a widow with three teenagers, in Kowalówka.

Paja and Shaya walked all night to get to Kowalówka, where they knocked on Mrs. Schwartz's door. She recognized them immediately, invited them in, and gave them some food. This time Shaya partook. Mrs. Schwartz peppered them with questions and they told her everything that had happened to them and their parents as they ate.

"Do not give up hope!" Mrs. Schwartz said. "You can stay with me this week, but you will have to move on after that. That's because I have workers who come to help me who are not as sympathetic as me. There are many good Poles who will help you. You know many of them."

Though well-intentioned and good-natured, Mrs. Schwartz's confidence in her neighbors' benevolence was grossly overstated. Others who used to shop at Jacob and Miriam Szlas' store refused to give their children refuge. Shaya and Paja knocked on several familiar doors only to be chased away, threatened, or both. With hiding places for two people seeming impossible, Shaya and Paja decided to separate and to meet every second week at Mrs. Schwartz's house.

After meeting with Paja twice in the span of a month, Shaya found a note addressed to him on his third visit to Mrs. Schwartz's in December 1942:

> *"Dear Brother: I found myself a job in the town of Srebna. I am working as a maid for a doctor's family and please don't worry about me. Just take care of yourself. Love, your sister Pola."*

By signing the note as "Pola," Paja was indicating that she had found refuge by hiding her Jewish identity and pretending to be Polish. Shaya happily took the note as a good sign that Paja would be able to wait out the war in relative comfort as a physician's nanny. Sounded like a plum job. With her blond hair and blue eyes, "Pola" was in a safe place, thought Shaya.

Shaya, on the other hand, was able to find a place to sleep by sneaking into various barns but had a hard time finding food. He would find stacks of hay, often lice-infested, to shield him from the bitter cold and eat snow. Months of sleeping in the haystacks without changing clothes gave him horrible rashes on his legs.

Author: Simply clean is not a way to describe the Schlosses' apartment. Shaya and Fay always kept their apartment pristinely immaculate. Looking back, Shaya remembered the filthy living conditions and always worked meticulously hard to overcompensate.

Sala Drexler
Prewar in Dąbrowa Górnicza

Approximately 5,000 Jews lived in Dąbrowa Górnicza (pronounced DAM-brov-a Gor-NEECH-a). There were big shuls and small shuls, there were Jewish committees and rabbis. People went to shul on Shabbat, people prepared on Friday. Chaskel and Bracha Drexler lived with their four children, Itzchak ("Itchik" and later "Irving"), Sala, Shifra, and Toba Leah in Dąbrowa Górnicza, approximately 85 kilometers west of Kraków near a smaller city of Katowice. Chaskel was a cattle-trader, selling cows to slaughterhouses. Before the war, the Drexlers had a nice, long table in their kitchen. They were a family of six people plus one – Bracha's single, younger sister, *Tanta* [Aunt] Esther, lived with them because Bracha and Esther's parents had both passed away.

Left to right: Itzchak, Bracha, Toba Leah, Chaskel, Sala, and Shifra Drexler.

The Drexlers tended chickens and some cows. Fresh eggs and milk were abundant. They lived on the same street as the local public school where Sala and her siblings attended until about two p.m. The two *shtiebels* [small synagogues] where Sala's father attended prayers and study were also down the block. Sala's brother went to cheder in nearby Bęndzin while she and her sisters went to a Bais Yaakov school for their Jewish education.

Nana: On Shabbat, Chaskel Drexler would bring home guests from shul for Shabbat meals. Bracha and the Drexler girls started preparing for the anticipated guests on Wednesday. On Wednesday, the fisherman would come around and Bracha bought live fish. Every Thursday, they bought flour and made challah from scratch. "There was no such thing that you could go and buy challah in a store. Everything was made from scratch. Even the noodles that we have – everything from scratch."

Sala recalled how her father made a living by trading cattle with anyone willing to do business, even those with prevalent antisemitism. "The Jew who made business with a non-Jew, that Polack would say and act like, 'My Jew is a good Jew, the rest are not. But my Jews, the ones I do business with, are good," she remembered. It helped that Chaskel's pleasant demeanor toward everyone made it easy for Jews and non-Jews alike to do business with him. They lived comfortably.

Bracha Drexler sponged up knowledge and readily shared her wisdom – she knew what it was like to be deprived of the opportunity to learn. Bracha had four sisters and two brothers. While her brothers learned in yeshiva, there was no Bais Yaakov school for girls in her town. But she wanted to learn so much that she actually sneaked into cheder to listen to how the boys learned – long before the film Yentl.

She was fluent in Polish and Yiddish. People who didn't know how to write letters came to Bracha for help. On Friday nights when Chaskel went to shul with Itchik, she would sit and read the *Tz'ena U'rena* – a weekly pamphlet of laws and stories geared toward women about the weekly parsha. She would also sing with her girls, recite *Tehillim* [chapters from the book of Psalms] together, and share her wisdom as they waited for Chaskel and Itchik to come home.

Sala had 50 girls in her public school class. The four Jews in class sat together but did not attend on Saturdays. Sometimes their classmates would share homework with them, but most times they did not, saying things like, "Why didn't you come to school? You're just being a lazy Jew!" Her classmates hated the Jews – some less pronounced and some more. Sala palpably felt the cold hate from her peers. She tried ignoring it as best she could, always taking the high road by ignoring whatever barbs were thrown her way.

Sala loved to sing. She sang with friends. She sang with her family. She also sang whatever songs she learned in public school. She often used her beautiful voice to soothe herself and those around her.

Nana Sala: I remember I had a friend whose parents had a store selling all kinds of paper goods for school. Her family name was Paraszol. In 1938, before the war broke out, they were such antisemites and already they listened to the radio about what Hitler was talking about the Jews. So the Polacks who sympathized with the Germans would not buy products from Jews and would stay by the Jewish stores and say to everyone about to go in: "Don't buy by the Jew, don't buy by the Jew." The Polacks said this. This attitude trickled down to the schoolyard too as the Paraszols would not let their daughter be friends with me anymore. We realized this clearly in 1938 – before September 1, 1939, when the war broke out. Hitler spoke on the radio preparing the Germans to scapegoat the Jews. He said, "If not for the Jews, things would be better for us." Everything was bad because of the Jews and they should be eliminated. "*Der Yuden zenen unser unglick.* [The Jew is our misfortune.]" This sentiment was in the air already. So things got very difficult right away when the war started. Everything went. Life was interrupted for Jews. Most Polacks were okay with this. Jews were not allowed to do anything. Right away, they were hunting Jews and catching them and sending some to work. Things became so bad that whatever was normal became abnormal. We had one room, and another room in our house we had to give to Polacks who were sympathizing with the Germans.

The Polacks were already against the Jews, even before the war.

On September 1, 1939, Sala was scheduled to start the new school year. The outbreak of war ended her formal education. It was a Friday morning when the Germans came on motorcycles and life changed overnight. They gave a list of things they wanted from the Jews. One day, it was fur coats, the next, jewelry and other expensive items. With each day that month came a new list of demands. Food was rationed and became scarce.

They restricted Jews from going to the city and ordered them to start wearing armbands. The Poles of Dąbrowa Górnicza were quite happy about it; in fact, they sought to ingratiate themselves with the Germans by helping identify their Jewish neighbors.

Nana Sala: Because, actually, if we did not wear the armbands and the Germans wouldn't see the armband, we could be okay. But if a Polack knew a Jew, right away they would give you up. For example, if a train came with rations of potatoes, every family would wait in line for a ration of potatoes. Starting from early in the morning, people would wait in line. So, my mother and father sent me to stay in line with my brother so we could get a couple potatoes. What do you think happened? Polacks on line would tell the Germans: "This is a Jew and this one's a Jew." And they pulled us off the line. No potatoes. This happened most days. It was very difficult.

The Germans' rationing and the Poles' penchant for tattling created a black market for goods overnight. Jews bartered with each other as much as they could to make ends meet.

Family Torn

As with Henyek Wimmer, Sala's brother, Itchik Drexler was forced to report to work in a factory. Itchik made tools for the Nazis there. On June 15, 1941, Itchik disappeared. He never came home from the factory that day. The SS showed up at the factory shortly after Itchik arrived, arrested him with some others, and took him.

Author: Nana Sala recalled Itchik's abduction in an interview with her great-grandson, Ori Schloss: "We did not know where he disappeared, where he went. Can you imagine the parents and the siblings of the boy, the son/brother who doesn't come home? He went out and he's not here anymore; and you don't hear from him, don't know what happened, except that we knew that people were randomly being sent to work in concentration camps. So we had hope he was alive. but it was terrible to live through. Terrible times but important to know."

Sally winced as she thought of her family's pain when Itchik went missing. Yet educating her 14-year-old great-grandson Ori Schloss about her brother (who survived the war) for a school project comforted her.

In the days and weeks following October 7, 2023, Sally remembered the loud motorcycles roaring into town on a random day as she and her family were going about their business in early September 1939. As any 13-year-old should be, she was looking forward to her first days of the new school year when the men on the motorcycles – and the hateful ideology that empowered them – changed her whole world forever. The near-looping videos on the news of the Hamas terrorists riding triumphantly into towns in southern Israel brought back the pain of those other bad men on bikes from decades earlier. She remembered Itchik being plucked off the streets and the pain of not knowing whether he was alive hiding somewhere, or dead, or worse. She remembered being cruelly separated from her parents and sisters, who were killed and denied proper burial. She heard that one of those abducted by Hamas was herself a Holocaust survivor. After an initial set of tears, Sally steeled herself and prayed: "Those families, I pray to God for those families." Always forward-thinking, Sally's tool of choice to combat evil was to step up her daily recitations of Psalms, a weapon of choice learned from her mother – praying for a peaceful resolution and a peaceful world.

Roundup in Dąbrowa Górnicza

Nana Sala: The Polish people delivered every family's name and how many children there were in each family to the Germans to curry favor. On August 12, 1942, the entire city's Jews were ordered to come to the marketplace with their whole families. So all the Jews of Dąbrowa Górnicza and surrounding villages came to our town where the marketplace was – a big open space. The SS people were all about. They were on the ground with rifles and on the roofs to watch to make sure nobody ran away from the place as everyone waited in line. The SS called each family to two tables at the front. As the SS called them, they knew in advance how many children the family had.

I was with my two young sisters (my brother was taken already) and my parents. My father was maybe 45, my mother was 43, and the two children were younger than I. So they said, "Parents and the two young children left." And me, I was 16, I had to go to the right. I don't know why. We didn't know when we separated that would be it – I never saw them again. So then, my mother's younger sister, Aunt Esther (who also was sent to the right), and I, we came back to the house, and what we did was just cry. As long as there were tears, we cried. A whole week. I was just 16 years old.

Concealed Defiance of a Seamstress Slave

Nana Sala: Where we went to school on my street, that became a sewing factory for the German soldiers' uniforms. I received a written work paper with my fingerprint on it, saying that I am working at the sewing factory. Men who were professional tailors cut the delivered materials, and the girls finished sewing the lining and the buttons. I did this from eight in the morning until six in the evening. At that time, Esther and I were chased out of our home like the Jews in Fiddler (on the Roof) from Anatevka. An uncle of ours helped us with a small wagon with basically whatever we could carry and brought it to the ghetto in Polna, which was further from the place we had to work than where I used to live with my family. We had to walk from the ghetto to report to the sewing factory in the morning. The school became known as one of Rossner's shops.

Alfred Rossner was a private German industrialist who contracted directly with the German SS to produce uniforms for the Nazi Wehrmacht. Making these uniforms was deemed essential for the German war effort, so the Jews who were forced to make them were given the protection of a special pass. For six months, Sala and her fellow workers walked back and forth from their homes in Dąbrowa Górnicza to Rossner's shop. (Although Sala did not know it at the time, the relatively decent conditions in the sewing factory were largely due to Rossner's personal touch. Rossner made sure his workers were humanely treated and risked his life to tip off Jews ahead of planned round ups. In December 1943, Rossner was executed by the Nazis for his efforts. Yad Vashem recognized Rossner as a "Righteous Among the Gentiles" in 1995.

"We sewed Nazi uniforms in Rossner's shop for six months. "And then," Sala said, "they took us to the concentration camp. Two hundred young girls, 16, 17, 18 years old, were needed to work in a factory.

They counted it out – Sala always stayed with her two friends Machusha and Balcza, and, luckily, all three were selected to go. The Germans allowed them to take a small pillow with them and not much else. Before leaving home, Sala realized she might not be going back. She grabbed a few articles of clothing. She grabbed two photos – the only ones she could find – one of her parents and one of only her mother. She quickly sewed a secret pocket into her flimsy sweater and stowed the photos inside. While her parents and siblings were always on her mind, she also defiantly kept her parents close to her heart in the only physical way she knew how. Keeping those photos with her throughout her ordeals gave Sala something tangible to latch onto to avoid losing hope. Keep going.

Before sending the 200 young women to a concentration camp, Sala and her group were sent to a labor camp in Gogolin, Poland. It was a filthy, crowded place where young, able-bodied men and women were taken before sending them off to work camps. Though some people were sent to work there, Sala and her friends waited there all day for four weeks before being sent to Gelanau near the Czechoslovakian border. When they arrived at Gelanau, they were the first to arrive; the barracks were clean. The facility was apparently built to service the nearby Christian Dierig weaving factory.

The machines at the Dierig weaving factory were complex. The group had to be taught how to use them properly – how to weave, thread the needles, fix the machines. They worked 12-hour shifts. One week they would work the 12-hour day shift, the next week they would work the 12-hour night shift. The factory was always buzzing to keep the German war machine going. The Germans allowed the group to wear the clothing they had brought with them; they did not give them prisoner uniforms because these forced laborers would be walking from barracks through a town to get to the factory. The Germans wanted to be able to show they were treating them humanely. It was good PR for the Dierig factory as well – if you want to call forced labor humane.

The women had to walk one hour each way to and from the barracks where they stayed to the factory where they worked. The barracks were crowded but at least they were cleaner than in Gogolin, Sala's prior camp. There was no hot water, but there was an oven in the middle that they used to heat themselves at night. They had wooden shoes, and the snow made it difficult to walk. German women with dogs supervised the daily march to and fro to keep the young ladies in line. At five a.m., a daily alarm went off in the barracks. Everyone had to stand in line and be counted. The Germans were obsessed with counting. They did not have numbers on their arms, but each person had one assigned to them. The SS woman would call a number and the prisoner had to loudly say they were present. They had a little bowl and had to stay in line and get some terrible soup for breakfast. There were sinks of cold water where they would wash themselves quickly if given time to do so.

Sala tried to keep her spirits up by humming to herself in her head when Germans were around and sang aloud when she could to boost others as well when the Germans left the prisoners to themselves. Because Sala's beautiful voice gave her fellow prisoners something pleasant, albeit fleeting under the circumstances, to get through the grinding day, she earned the title of kanarek – Polish for canary. The canary is a small, beautiful bird, often kept in a cage, that sings.

Sala and her group of 200 were in Gelenau for over a year. Then they were transferred to a bigger camp called Langenbielau. It was run by the same Dierig conglomerate but had 1,000 young ladies. Nasty female German guards took pleasure in yelling at them and in the occasional beatdown as they counted workers before marching them off to the factory where they would sew uniforms all day.

There, Sala and her fellow slave laborers made the crisp Nazi uniforms of death's agents. Sala drew her strength to continue by relying on her fellow workers, all clad in the same prison uniform. However, Sala's sweater which she had been allowed to keep, had a unique component from which she drew inspiration. The photo of her parents secretly sewn into her pocket kept her parents and everything they stood for close to Sala's heart.

That same photo has remained at Sala's bedside for over seven decades.

The Pastors' Place
"Stay with Us Shaya (But Don't Tell Mr. Pastor!)"

Shaya racked his brain trying to remember which of his parents' customers might still be grateful enough – and compassionate enough – to allow him to hide out for a bit. He remembered the Pastors, an elderly couple with grown children. Some were married and living with them. On a freezing December night in 1942, Shaya found his way to their front door. He could see the whole family eating in the kitchen, huddling around a burning stove. Shaya timidly knocked and Mrs. Pastor warmly invited him in. As the Pastors' children peppered Shaya with questions such as, "Where have you been?" and "What happened to your family?" Mr. Pastor remained silent with his arms folded, grimacing an old-man grimace to indicate he clearly was taking no part in the hospitality his family was extending. Mrs. Pastor warmed up some soup and invited Shaya to eat. The Pastors confided in Shaya that they knew of some Jews hiding in nearby villages as Mr. Pastor shook his head disapprovingly. After an hour or so of talking about current events, Mr. Pastor went to sleep. The others then let Shaya in on a more personal secret.

"Our Dad has no clue," said one of the Pastor children as another stifled a short giggle.

"Your cousins are hiding in our barn, wanna see them?" The oldest Pastor son led Shaya to the barn where Shaya's cousin Goldy, her husband Efraim Epstein, Shaya's cousin Shmulke, and another young couple were hiding, and he then left. Goldy and Shmulke were the children of Shaya's mother's cousin. Shaya and the group compared their tales of woe – the cousins had so many brushes with death and near misses that they were content to stay in the barn. The Pastors were good people who brought them food. As long as they stayed down when Mr. Pastor came around, they would try to ride out the war in this space. They had grown tired of running and this seemed like their surest route to survival.

"Stay with us, Shaya," they said. Finally, a safe place to rest and have others to rely on, he initially thought. "Stay with us, Shaya." Yet the more he contemplated staying in one place, the less comfortable he felt with the idea. No matter how genuine or safe at the moment, the space and logistical constraints involved in adding a sixth person to an already-cramped hiding space made it an unlikely place to hunker down indefinitely.

"But where is your baby?" Shaya asked Goldy and Efraim, wishing he had bit down hard on his tongue before asking. Their pained look said all that needed to be said. Shaya immediately realized he should not have uttered those words and felt horrible for even asking. He remembered that the last time he had seen Goldy was shortly after she gave birth to a beautiful baby girl sometime in 1940. He remembered how happily Goldy and Efraim doted on their daughter.

With tears, they told Shaya how she died. While lying hidden in a barn, they saw through peepholes that some German soldiers were passing by just as the baby started to cry. Goldy and Efraim panicked. Goldy tried calming the baby down but could not. Efraim covered the baby's mouth to stifle the noise. Tragically, the crying stopped, along with the baby's breathing. Permanently.

"Will you stay with us, Shaya?" they persisted. But how could he stay? As nice as the Pastors were, it was only a matter of time, Shaya figured, before the Pastor children would become unable to hide and feed another person safely. Case in point was Goldy and Efraim's baby.

"Keep running!" Shaya heard his mother's voice telling him.

Seeking Refuge with Familiar Faces in No-Longer-Safe Spaces

Shaya decided to keep moving every few days to avoid wearing out the welcome of those who actually welcomed him and not to become so entrenched in one place that he aroused suspicion. On Christmas Day 1942, Shaya found another family, the Kachorowskis – a couple and two young children who had been customers of his parents. "Oh, Jesus! Look who came to join us today!" Mr. Kachorowski exclaimed with a tinge of religious fervor as he saw Shaya on his porch and invited him in. The whole family lived in one large room – kitchen, living room, and bedroom rolled into one. The Kachorowskis asked essentially the same questions the Pastors had and, with each answer, marveled at the divine providence that brought Shaya to their home.

"God obviously sent you here to be with us today," Mr. Kachorowski said. "We have to help you. Stay with us and we will teach you the way of Christ." Mrs. Kachorowski fixed up something for him to sleep on.

"No, it's too much trouble for you; I can sleep in the barn," Shaya said.

"Don't worry, there's plenty of room for you here, and it is way too cold for you to sleep outside," Mr. Kachorowski said. He then gave him something he hadn't had in years – clean underwear and pajamas – and took his clothes to disinfect. With every small favor, Mr. Kachorowski reminded Shaya about Christ in some way.

"He was a big Christian fanatic and he asked me to convert after the war would be finished," Shaya later recalled.

He had no intention of converting but saw that by helping out the Kachorowskis, he might just survive. He couldn't remember the last time he had slept anywhere without having to worry about cold, vermin, animals, or being found, let alone having a warm bed.

Shaya helped out with as many chores as possible as Mr. Kachorowski proudly believed he was in the process of converting a Jew. "Remember the Szlas family that used to have that grocery store?" Mr. Kachorowski eagerly asked his friends and relatives at church as a lead-in to some juicy gossip. "Their son is helping us out on the farm and is converting!" He was shocked to learn that they were not as excited about harboring a Jew as he was.

"But he's converting!"

"You're hiding a Jew and putting us all at risk!" Mr. Kachorowski's brother scolded him. "You get rid of that Jew from your house right now or I'll do it for you."

Mr. Kachorowski came home from church shaken from being berated by his friends and brother and told Shaya to leave. Immediately.

"I'm sorry," he said, "but too many people know you're here, and we're all at risk."

They wouldn't have known so fast if you had just kept your mouth shut, thought Shaya. Hoping to come back for a night or two in the future if needed, he decided not to burn bridges as he thanked the Kachorowskis and left.

Though two weeks of living like a human came to an abrupt end, he left the Kachorowskis with renewed determination to keep going. He figured that the Pastors', where his cousins were, and Mrs. Schwartz's place, where he had met his sister, were relatively safe places he could go to for a few days at a time while hoping for some good fortune in between.

January 1943 was bitterly cold, so Shaya couldn't be shy. He knocked on several doors of farmers he did not know, only to be turned away abruptly by the polite ones and threatened by those who were more blunt. Few were as sympathetic as Mrs. Schwartz, who allowed him to stay in a barn for a few days at a time. But even Mrs. Schwartz grew weary of being put out after cycling back to her a second or third time in early 1943. By then, he largely hid in barns without telling the owners, digging himself into a pile of straw or hay. It was barely enough to shield him from the elements, and he could feel himself running a high fever. He tried resting it off, but without food, it would be a matter of time before hunger and the elements would do him in. It would have been easier for Shaya to simply lie there. And he thought about it, too. But again, he mustered strength from his mother's words to keep moving, weak but determined, and made his way to the Pastors.

He found the Pastor family to be the most benevolent. Unfortunately, they could barely feed themselves, let alone provide for the five Jews they were hiding. When Shaya went back to the Pastors to see his cousins, the couple who had been hiding with them was gone. They had left to search for food one night and never came back. Unlike Mr. Kachorowski, the Pastors hid Jews discreetly, so they were privy to the neighborhood gossip and discovered what happened. A Polish farmer from the next town caught the couple trying to steal an animal from his farm. He killed them.

The Pastors understood the risk but nonetheless allowed Shaya's cousins to hide out. Every third day or so, his cousins would sneak out at night to steal an animal from a farm. The Pastors would then prepare the food and share it. Shaya's cousins shared whatever meager provisions they had with Shaya. He beat the fever and regained his strength after about a week.

One stormy night, he joined his cousins as they scouted farms in the neighboring village. Armed with a large knife and a few empty sacks, Shaya and his cousins found a pig pen, killed the pig, cut it into quarters, and carried it back to the Pastors, who were able to cook the meat for several days' worth of food.

For the next two weeks, he stayed with his cousins and helped them dig an underground shelter in the barn. A few weeks prior, some German soldiers had randomly searched houses in the area, including the Pastors'. Luckily, they only glanced into the barn where Shaya's cousins were lying still in the dark before moving on. The cousins needed an underground space that could be concealed to avoid detection. After finishing the new hiding space, Shaya felt it was time to move on. As is, there were enough mouths to feed and the small space was a bit tight. He decided to risk going back to his hometown of Jasiniec the next day. Perhaps an old classmate he had been somewhat friendly with would help him for a few days.

Just as he was plotting out his course, one of the Pastor boys ran to the barn. "Get to your underground shelter, fast!" he said. "Germans are next door!" They opened the door to the underground shelter and jumped inside as the Pastor boy covered it up with some heavy equipment. The underground hideout was about four feet high. As soon as the door closed, "Squish!" The area had about a foot of water. They heard noise above and dared not move as they sat in it. The door was airtight and they had no ventilation. After the noise subsided, Shaya and his cousins tried opening the door but could not. They did not want to pound on the door lest the Germans hear it and come back. Again, Shaya thought he was breathing his last breath, thinking he had let his family down.

After a few hours with little air, they all grew weary. Thankfully, the Pastor boy returned and let them out just before they all blacked out. Gasping for air but grateful for life, Shaya made up his mind on the spot to continue to keep moving. *Too close of a brush with death,* he thought. *I'm just as safe out there. The safe room isn't safe. Who knows if the Pastors will be able to let us out in time next time?*

He wished his cousins well and left within a few hours. Roaming the Polish countryside before dawn, he found a small home, quietly opened an unlocked front door, and stole some bread sitting on a kitchen table. The bread held him over for a day or so before making his way to his old public school classmate Janek's house in Jasiniec. Janek and Shaya sat near each other in public school class. Janek was not exactly a friend, but they had played in the schoolyard together at times and was never outwardly mean toward Shaya like many of the others. Shaya made his way to Janek's house and peeked through the front window. Janek and his mother were sitting in the kitchen as Shaya knocked. "How are you still alive? How did you get here?" Janek peppered him excitedly with questions as if seeing an old friend.

"Long story, happy to tell you everything," he said, thrilled at the warm greeting. "I'm very hungry. Would you be able to share some bread?"

"We have not a single crumb in our house, Shaya, but we're baking tomorrow. If you come back tomorrow evening, we can give you a whole loaf."

"Thank you so much! I will see you then!"

Shaya found an unlocked barn nearby and stayed there overnight thinking about the fresh bread he'd have tomorrow. He snacked on some wheat seeds he found and went to sleep in a good mood. One day at a time meant one day closer to the end of the war. With enough people around like Janek willing to share a bit, he liked his chances. Shaya stayed in the barn all next day before heading back for the bread.

Shaya wondered how he would thank Janek and his mother, hoping to periodically barter services for some food. As Shaya approached

Janek's house, he did not immediately notice that several people were inside the house. "Hey, so glad you came," Janek said with a grin. "I'm sure the police will be very happy to see you, too." With that, four of Janek's friends, some of whom Shaya recognized, bolted out the front door and attempted to grab him. He swung his arms wildly and even landed a punch as he miraculously ran away from Janek's front yard. So much for the old schoolyard chum.

Covering For Romek Wimmer's Broken Leg

By 1944, the Allied forces had started to bomb some of the factories known to be part of the German war machine. Rumors spread that the Germans would soon be moving the workers to a new camp. In advance of being moved out, some Poles with ties to the Polish underground and several Jews decided to attempt to break out of Stalowa Wola. Given his plum position in the infirmary, Romek was given a note to pass along to a Pole named Biernat about the logistics of the plan. There would be an explosion from outside, and anyone who could, should run to the nearby forest. As Romek started on his way to deliver the message to Biernat that evening, an alarm sounded and all the lights went out because the factory was being bombed. Romek hastily jumped down some steps as the alarm blared and broke his leg as he landed.

Unable to walk or run, Romek was still determined to deliver the note with the plan's logistics to Biernat. He moved along, wincing in pain, as he found Biernat. Biernat confirmed that the Germans would be moving all the workers out of the plant to another location. The transition presented an opportune time to escape. However, seeing that Romek could barely move, Biernat used a makeshift stretcher and took him back to the barracks with a few others. "Good luck, and thank you for delivering this," said a physician, Dr. Goldenberg, who set Romek's leg in plaster.

"It's the only way you're going to heal," the doctor told Romek. "It needs to be set."

The next morning, as planned, approximately 100 people ran away from Stalowa Wola. Romek stayed behind, wishing he hadn't broken his leg and wondering whether his broken leg might also mean a death sentence. Thankfully for Romek, the breakout diverted the Germans' anger and attention toward trying to retrieve those who had escaped. Romek lay low with Dr. Goldenberg's help and that of his friends.

Though the war was starting to turn against the Germans by then, the SS did not take kindly to a large percentage of the workforce fleeing to the forest. As soon as they found out about it, they followed in hot pursuit. Because these were skilled munitions workers, and Germany needed more munitions, the workers who were found were not killed. They were brought back and beaten up badly enough to make a point, but not badly enough to preclude them from working. Some evaded capture and were eventually liberated by the Russians. (Some, like Romek's friend Sam Poznanski's brother, were conscripted by the Russian army. Poznanski's brother died in battle fighting the Germans in Berlin under the Russian flag.)

The remaining workers were transported to Plaszów, a massive work camp surrounded by barbed wire fences divided into multiple areas. There were factories, warehouses, a men's camp, a women's camp, and a "labor education camp" for Poles who had violated labor rules.

As Romek's leg was in a cast, he was brought to the infirmary at Plaszów. Though it was a work camp, random shootings happened with frequency there. Every few days, the SS would come to the infirmary and select people who could not work to be shot. Romek needed some *protektzia* [protection], which Dr. Goldenberg sought out. His friend, Dr. Lefkowitz, ran the infirmary. "Please, Dr. Lefkowitz, watch this guy, he's like my little brother." Dr. Goldenberg said. There were some close calls in the first three weeks as Dr. Lefkowitz hid Romek during a ew inspections.

The Jewish leader in Plaszów was a man named Goldstein who had been transferred from Stalowa Wola with Romek. He became the Lager after the Germans killed the previous one to randomly instill fear among the workers soon after the workers from Stalowa Wola had arrived. Goldstein knew Romek well and wanted to avoid his predecessor's fate. "How much time does he need to heal?" Goldstein asked the doctors.

"About another three weeks," they answered.

"Romek, you can't stay here. Eventually, they'll kill you and possibly others if they find out we've been covering for you. I'm sending you to the brush factory. You'll work at a machine where you can sit most of the time." After a few weeks of working in the brush factory, Goldstein rotated Romek to a more rigorous job, enabling someone more needy by then to work while sitting.

As 1944 progressed, the SS unleashed their anger about losing the war on the workers with more frequency. That meant random shooting and more bodies to dispose of. Romek and the others did their assigned jobs and then were tasked with the grisly job of digging pits and bringing the bodies to those pits where the Germans could burn them. The awful smell of death permeated the Plaszów work camp.

The writing was on the wall as the killings became more frequent; the prisoners understood it was likely a matter of time before those forced to bury others might soon be buried themselves. Nonetheless, the remaining workers plugged away, giving each other support when possible. Having each other's backs was the only viable path toward survival.

Oskar Schindler's famous enamelware factory was in Kraków, adjacent to the Plaszów camp. Schindler convinced the Germans to move the factory to Czechoslovakia, further away from the brunt of the fighting, both to preserve his business and to save over 1,000 Jews from being deported to a death camp. The Germans also decided to move some other workers out of Plaszów, too. Romek heard about the pending move of Schindler's factory and wanted out. Goldstein told Romek that some workers would be staying. Those not going with Schindler's factory would go to Gross-Rosen, a nearby industrial work camp. Romek didn't care where, but he wanted out of Plaszów. Goldstein put Romek on the list for Gross-Rosen: the devil you don't know can't be worse than the hell that was Plaszów. Or could it?

Say it Confidently and You'll Just Learn on the Job

In November 1944, with snow on the ground, Romek and a few hundred others were taken – naked – to Gross-Rosen, a vast industrial complex with dozens of sub camps. They stood outside for a while until they were told to go to the barracks. Romek recognized a familiar face from his hometown, a man named Wassenberg, who gave him some precious advice.

"Tomorrow, when the Nazis come to register you, tell them that you are a mechanic," Wassenberg said. "They need as many mechanics as possible." He knew that Romek was no mechanic. "Say it confidently and you'll just learn on the job."

Two days later, Nazi officers registered them, taking down names and professions. Romek took Wassenberg's advice and newly minted himself as a mechanic.

Author: Later in life, Papa Romek used Wassenberg's advice many times and in different business contexts. He never shied away from taking on business, even if it may have been slightly out of his comfort zone. Project confidence to get the business, then work as hard as needed to figure out how to deliver.

Sure enough, 100 people who registered as "mechanics" were given new uniforms and taken from Gross-Rosen on trucks to the subcamp Reichenbach. It had nicer, newer, relatively clean barracks. When Romek arrived, he started asking around, "Did anyone here come from Stalowa Wola, Plaszów, or Rozwadów?"

"A group of people originally from Wieliczka, Kraków, and Rozwadów came from there a few weeks ago," someone replied. Music to Romek's ears! So he started playing Jewish geography and rattled off names of his friends from his hometown area who were with him in his prior camps, hoping to find someone he knew.

"Shlemek Poznanski?"

"Sure. He's in Block two."

Romek ran over to Block two to meet his good friend. Shlemek had assumed that Romek did not survive the broken leg. After a joyous reunion – as joyous as could be in a forced slave labor camp – Shlemek gave Romek some bread he had saved and explained the camp's routines and what to avoid. They worked together making ammunition for the Luftwaffe, the German air force. With Shlemek's help, Romek learned how to use the machinery and was never called out for his lack of formal training.

The Two Russian Troublemakers

Any time he crossed paths with other Jews in hiding, Shaya swapped stories and survival strategies. The people he found hiding in barns generally had one strategy: find a safe spot and try to wait out the war. More than a few times, he found out that people he had met were eventually turned in by the same farmers who had hidden them. As much as he would have liked to stay with others for more than a few days, Shaya knew it was too dangerous, both from experience and his mother's gut-wrenching last words to him. Shaya found constant solace in his mother's wisdom and plea to keep moving and trained himself to keep an eye out for possible next steps.

As the weather began to thaw in April 1943, Shaya found it easier to move around. He didn't need to sleep indoors as much and ventured into the nearby forests. One night while deep in the forest, Shaya smelled fire. He followed the scent and saw a man tending to a small campfire. As he got closer, he recognized that the man was from Ostrów, where his family had lived. Anshel Wojsniak recognized Shaya, too, and they shared their stories. Like Shaya, Anshel had been on the run. Anshel and his brother found different ways to be useful to certain locals. Anshel's brother worked as a shepherd for a Polish farmer, tending to a flock of sheep. Anshel periodically visited his brother in the stable. Anshel sometimes helped that farmer, too. The small fire in the forest, for instance, was actually a crude way to manufacture whiskey. The farmer came the next day with some food in exchange for the home-made whiskey.

That night, two Russian soldiers who had escaped from a German war prison chanced upon Anshel and Shaya. They politely explained how they were caught, how they escaped, and that they now needed help. "Come join us," they said. "We'll help you get some revenge and make some money in the process."

"How?" Shaya asked incredulously.

"With guns."

"How are we going to get guns?" Shaya asked again with even more skepticism.

"For money," they matter-of-factly replied.

The circular reasoning didn't bother Shaya as much as their nonchalant confidence. Shaya sensed something was not right about these soldiers.

"Okay, maybe not with money exactly," one of them continued. "Plenty of Jews left possessions with some of the locals. We all know that even if someone hid a Jewish family for a while, by now, that farmer has turned. The goods are still there; the Jews they may have been hiding in their attic or barn are likely long gone by now."

Now he's starting to make sense, thought Shaya.

"If you two are still here, you guys must know of a few Poles who have it coming to them."

Indeed, Shaya knew of a Jewish family whom he had come across. They had hidden with a Polish family until they found the Jews to be too much of a burden.

Before hitting up that farm, the Russians wanted to show Anshel and Shaya how easy it was to get some food. "Pick up some sticks and let's go to the next farmhouse we see." When they got to the first farmhouse, the Russians told Anshel and Shaya to go to the backyard and start making lots of noise: screaming, banging the sticks around, whatever they could do to make it sound like there were many people. The Russians banged in the front door and started roughing up the frightened farmer. One put him in a headlock.

"Lie down on the floor and call your wife down here and we won't kill you," they said.

The wife came down immediately and started begging the Russians not to kill them. "We'll give you whatever you want! Just please don't hurt us!"

"Go get us some loaves of bread and strings of kielbasa," they ordered. She quickly did and handed a bundle of food to the Russian who was not holding her husband.

"Thank you very much," said the Russian matter-of-factly. "And if you tell anyone that Russians were here and we find out, we will burn this house to the ground with you in it. Have a nice evening!" And with that, they left the petrified couple alone.

"See? Easy!" said one Russian as he led Shaya and Anshel to a new hiding place in the forest. They feasted on the kielbasa and loaves of bread together as the Russians explained how they would approach the next target. Shaya knew the farm they would be going to and how to get there, so he was to lead the way. While in hiding about a year earlier, Shaya had seen the farmer unload what seemed like all of a Jewish family's valuable possessions from a wagon and bring them up to an attic above the barn.

Shaya came across the Jewish family one night, who explained they had made a deal with the farmer to hide them in exchange for their valuables. They invited Shaya to stay with them, and he did for a few nights to get out of the bitter cold. But Shaya sensed correctly that their hideout in the barn would not last. He moved on and the family was turned in not long after.

Once they got to the barn, Anshel and one of the Russians would wait at the front door with big sticks. The sticks were in case the farmer would need to be subdued as Shaya and the other Russian took as many goods as possible from the barn attic.

The Russian climbed the ladder, filled four sacks with everything he could as quickly and quietly as possible, and threw them down to Shaya. Each of them carried away a sack of goods and made it back to their hiding place in the forest before sunrise.

They opened the sacks in the morning to find expensive fur coats, new silks, and fine cotton goods. "Tonight, we'll take some of this and sell it to farmers. With that money, we'll buy guns. See how simple that was?"

The Russian's words did not comfort Shaya. The Cheshire cat-like grin and tone of voice made Shaya nervous that the scheme would put him at risk. Shaya instinctively wanted to part ways but could not verbalize his concern to Anshel in front of the Russians. At nightfall, the Russians started to gather some of the goods, so Shaya and Anshel followed their lead. Suddenly, the Russians both pulled out knives, saying, "You aren't taking anything." Anshel immediately bolted, leaving Shaya alone with the two Russians.

"Please, just let me go. Take all of the goods, just let me go, please," Shaya pleaded. The Russians laughed and let him go.

With each step Shaya took as he ran away from the Russians, he grew more furious with Anshel. He found Anshel in one of his go-to spots and gave him a piece of his mind. "How could you have abandoned me like that?!" It was more of a rhetorical indictment than a question. He expected no satisfactory answer from Anshel because he already knew the truth. When confronted, Anshel instinctively fled, leaving him to fight off the Russian brigands alone. In fact, after getting his anger with Anshel off his chest, Shaya left him. Better to rely on yourself than a fair-weather friend who did not have your back. Shaya remained determined to move on by himself with his own wits.

Eugenius Dienciol "Geniek"

By May 1943, the Jews who had been hiding in barns and attics were venturing out more than they had during the colder weather. Polish antisemites fancied it a bit of a sport to find and kill a Jew. It was good for bragging rights at church as well as the local tavern. Every time Shaya heard about a Jew being found and killed, he wondered whether he would be next. He did not harp on it, though, as his mother's words rang constantly in his head and girded him to fight for as long as he could. Though determined, he felt very alone.

It had been a while since he stopped by Mrs. Schwartz's, where he and his sister had met about a year earlier. His sister Paja had left him a note indicating she had taken on a non-Jew's identity and was working for a Polish doctor's family. He was certain that Mrs. Schwartz would have some updates on Paja. Thankfully, Mrs. Schwartz invited Shaya to stay in the barn for a few days and indeed had regards from Paja for him. "She's doing well there," Mrs. Schwartz said. "They do not know she is Jewish."

Mrs. Schwartz had a young Polish teenager named Eugenius Dienciol working for her to help around the farm. Mrs. Schwartz sent Eugenius, nicknamed "Geniek," to the barn with food, and Shaya struck up a conversation with him. Geniek was an orphaned teenager with blond hair, blue eyes, thin build, and about 1.75 meters tall (five feet, nine inches). Mrs. Schwartz sympathized with Geniek as her children had grown up fatherless, and Geniek happily took whatever work she could give him. He appreciated Shaya's conversation. As Shaya relaxed in Mrs. Schwartz's barn that night, thinking of Paja and her experience, he realized a smarter way to survive.

When Geniek delivered some milk and bread to Shaya the next morning, he asked Geniek: "Do you have identification papers?"

"Yes."

"Can I see them?"

"Sure."

It had no photo, just Geniek's physical description and thumbprint.

Perfect, thought Shaya, who was also blond, blue-eyed, thin build, and about 1.75 meters tall. "You're staying here with Mrs. Schwartz for a while?" he asked.

"Yes, I help her and she takes care of me."

Shaya mustered whatever small amount of money he had in his pocket from his venture out with the Russians and convinced a willing Geniek to trade an identification card for the small amount of cash.

The Schwerdreskis Find a Great Worker

Shaya came up with a good story to match his new ID card. He, "Geniek," would tell farmers whose doors he knocked on that he was orphaned shortly after the war broke out and that he, a Polish Catholic teenager, was looking for work and a place to stay to ride out the war. Shaya hiked a few miles in a direction where he was not familiar with the locals. He found that "Geniek" was greeted much more warmly than Shaya was when knocking on strangers' doors. Shaya felt somewhat safer as he saw how well the plausible ruse seemed to work. Of course, the threshold was fairly low, given that no one who answered the door chased him away, threatened to beat him, or turned him in. Rather, his tale of wartime woe was met only with sympathy and genuine concern. After knocking on the doors of a few farmhouses with this story, Shaya learned that the Schwerdreski family down the road needed some help.

He found the Schwerdreski's farm – adult children living with their widowed mother. After he told his story and explained all the farm tasks he could do, the oldest son, Cheslaw, hired him on the spot. He knew his way around a farm and worked like a horse; he did the work of three people. Cheslaw and his siblings were thrilled with Shaya and saw his arrival as a welcome blessing from above. Shaya worked hard to routinize his chores and invested his entire being into working hard. Mrs. Schwerdreski washed Shaya's clothes once a week and the food was plentiful. Shaya's lice, rashes, and hunger faded away. Living as a non-Jew, he began to believe that his and his sister Paja's chances of surviving were good.

Cheslaw happily delegated his duties as head of the farm to this workhorse and made himself scarce. Apparently, Cheslaw held a position in the Polish underground. With "Geniek" helping out at the family farm, Cheslaw dedicated his time almost exclusively to his side hustle. As the months went by, Shaya learned more and more about the Polish underground's objectives and Cheslaw's activities. Cheslaw helped train other Poles to get ready to free Poland from German occupation. They spent the nights patrolling villages, when the remaining Jews in hiding came out to search for food. They convinced themselves that hunting hungry Jews was a type of military training. He was secretly petrified of being caught, but his cover story, as "Geniek" coupled with his hard work at the farm, helped Shaya stay largely under the radar.

One day, Cheslaw called Shaya into a meeting inside the Schwerdreski home with about a dozen others. *They know. they're going to kill me*, thought Shaya. He recalled his classmate Janek's ruse with the fictional bread, except Janek only had four relatively scrawny people with him. Shaya's heart beat fast as he scanned the room full of able-bodied men. Someone older than Cheslaw, a leader in the Polish underground, started the meeting, addressing Shaya: "Cheslaw tells us that you are a hard worker and a good Polish Catholic," he said. "If we need to call on you for help, we trust that you will fight with us. Will you?"

"Of course," he answered, relieved.

"You swear allegiance?"

"Yes, I swear."

"Okay, Geniek. Do not tell any neighbors about our group. We just need to make sure you understand that you need to cooperate if we need you. You can go back to your work now." And with that, the leader raised a cup and drank to everyone's good health and good luck, and the meeting continued without Shaya.

Though glad that Cheslaw had unknowingly fortified his "Geniek" identity, Shaya remained queasy and cautious about hiding in plain sight. The frequent stories he overheard from Cheslaw, his friends, and the other Schwerdreskis about finding and killing Jews left Shaya in a quandary. On one hand, the cover story solidly worked for him. On the other, though he was several kilometers away from the small towns and villages he knew, he couldn't help but imagine that it was only a matter of time before an old classmate or other acquaintance would show up as a member of Cheslaw's group.

Ghoulish Gossip

One day, Mrs. Schwerdreski returned from visiting a friend as Shaya was cleaning up. She told her family a story about a young, light-haired Jewish woman who was working for a family in the village of Srebrna. A doctor's family. His heart sank as his mind started to race again, hoping he was only imagining what he was hearing. He wasn't.

"For many months!"

The family gasped in horror as Mrs. Schwerdreski continued: "And when the doctor found out, he called the Polish police, who turned her over to the Germans." She sounded like she was telling a joke leading up to a morbid punchline. "And then the Germans took her to a cemetery and shot her right there! Convenient, no?" ending her story in a cackle of laughter from all present as Shaya pretended not to have heard from the next room.

Everything about Mrs. Schwerdreski's delivery shook Shaya to his core. Mrs. Schwerdreski had been washing his clothes, feeding him, and providing room and board for many months; he thought her to be a kind person who unfortunately became a widow at a young age. He wanted to believe that under other circumstances, his parents might have allowed her to run up a tab at their grocery store or found other ways to help her out. Shaya bit his tongue hard as he worked through his chores faster and harder. "Keep a straight face or they'll know!" he kept telling himself. As the Schwerdreskis laughed at the murder of the young woman in the Srebrna doctor's home, Shaya kept a straight face and kept busy. No *shiva* [traditional seven-day mourning period]. No burial. No mourning rituals. Just a private scream inside himself as he plowed through his chores with the stiffest of an upper lip. He refused to let himself process the profound grief over learning that his light haired, Jewish sister Paja had just been murdered. "Geniek" had no reason to mourn, so he could not.

About a week later, he found himself alone working in the field on a chilly, windy day. "*Ayeka* [Where are you]?!" Shaya screamed, knowing that no one but God himself could hear him. "Ayeka?!"

Author: Shaya knew that this one Hebrew word, "Ayeka," was loaded with meaning. Shaya's deeply pious father had taught him the story of Adam and Eve in the Garden of Eden. Right after partaking of the forbidden fruit, the world's first couple tried to hide from God. "Where are you – Ayeka?" he asked the guilty pair. Of course, God knew precisely where Adam and Eve were but nonetheless tried drawing them out with dialogue. That one word conveyed a query having nothing to do with physical location. Rather, it was loaded to convey disappointment. The "Where are you" was meant to trigger some introspection: "Look where you are now compared to where you were. What you have done is so far beneath you. You two had the world at your fingertips and you blew it. How could you? One rule! And you couldn't control yourselves. Ayeka!"

Grandpa Shaya, then a young man with an uncertain future and no family, vented to God himself. Where was He? Shaya's parents and siblings were pious people. Good, kind people. How could You? Where are YOU now?

It took several decades, but I believe that Grandpa Shaya eventually found an answer that satisfied him. In 2007, Grandpa joined us for Simchas Torah , a holiday that celebrates the yearly cycle of reading one section of the Torah each week. Grandpa stood in the back of the shul pensively taking in the scene of Jews two, three, even four generations his junior, singing and dancing with the shul's Torahs and with each other. He slowly took in the scene of hundreds of Jewish children and their parents, grandparents, and even some other great-grandparents celebrating the festive holiday together.

"Grandpa, is everything okay?" I asked.

He answered me quickly but kept his gaze on the beautiful scene in front of him. "You think, maybe, there might be some children of some Holocaust survivors here?"

"Of course. I'd estimate that over half of the families here have at least one survivor grandparent on one side. Most probably have more than one."

Shaya looked around the busy room again slowly and said with a quiet sigh, soft smile, and a raised eyebrow, "They didn't win, Tatele." And again, he repeated to me, but also to himself in quiet wonder, "Tatele, they didn't win." (*Tatele* is Yiddish for "little Daddy, a term of endearment)

What was far from clear while screaming "Ayeka" in Mrs. Schwerdreski's field became clearer to him in this setting as he reflected not only on what he had built, but on the rebuilt Jewish communities in the decades that followed. God was always there, and while things looked very bleak, they didn't win. When a grandfather who has seen a large part of the arc of Jewish history play out before his eyes can look around in a packed shul and softly declare victory to his grandson, that's the answer to "Ayeka." Grandpa was a living testament that defied the odds. He made deliberate choices to never give up, always remembering his mother's plea to keep running. All the small choices added up over time. To move on, to build a family with my dear grandma, he correctly stated the obvious on that Simchas Torah day in shul. They didn't win.

Vigilance Needed at All Times

With the prospect of ever meeting his sister at Mrs. Schwartz's again dashed, Shaya felt like giving up more than he ever had. He was tired of being "Geniek" and the constant self-vigilance needed to avoid detection. He could not shed a tear or act unusually in any way. The specter of his mother's desperate exhortation to keep running kept him from giving in to the mental exhaustion of his situation.

Shortly after he learned of Paja's murder, the Schwerdreski family started to prepare for a party for some kind of family milestone. Many friends, neighbors, and extended family descended on the Schwerdreski farm to celebrate with plentiful food and liquor. Shaya preferred to be the one serving drinks so he did not have to drink himself. A cousin of the Schwerdreskis worked on Shaya to get him drunk, cajoling him to down several shots of whiskey. After the party, some relatives, including the cousin, stayed over to sleep it off. Though buzzed and tired, Shaya tucked himself into his own bed without bothering to undress and fell asleep. In the middle of the night, he felt tugging at his pants' zipper. The cousin who had plied Shaya with whiskey was curious to see if "Geniek" was a Jew. Shaya turned over on his stomach, pretending to still be asleep, and the cousin gave up trying, fell asleep himself, and thankfully left the next morning.

By October 1943, Shaya had spent more time at the Schwerdreski farm than any other single place since that fateful post-Yom Kippur evening in 1941 when his mother urged him to leave with his friends. Should he keep running just because of one drunk cousin's overtures? No, he rationalized. He was hard-working Geniek, an indispensable asset to the Schwerdreski farm. He worked so hard and meticulously that the Schwerdreskis would not want to suspect anything even if they did. So Shaya stayed put, albeit resigned to remain vigilant.

Russians Again

In October 1943, Cheslaw Schwerdreski tapped Shaya to help chop wood for the upcoming winter's firewood. They took a horse and wagon to the forest and cut down some trees. As they were resting, Shaya saw two familiar figures in uniform and rifles on their back approaching – the same Russian soldiers who had forced him to join them in raiding farms for food and supplies. Shaya had no way of knowing if they would blow his cover and, again, his heart raced.

When they approached, one engaged Cheslaw in conversation while the other winked at Shaya who winked back. They chatted up Cheslaw a bit more and remained cordial, again gesturing to Shaya on the sly to indicate that his secret was safe for now. They left without incident. On the way back to the Schwerdreskis' farm, Cheslaw explained to Shaya how he knew them. They were all on the same "team" of sorts for now. They had escaped from a German prison camp and worked at a neighboring farm with others who had escaped. Another Polish farmer tipped off the Germans to curry some favor. Some of the Russian soldiers were recaptured. Others, like these two, used their military training to successfully evade capture and regrouped in the forest in small two-to-three-person units. These Russians knew Cheslaw to be a ranking member of the Polish underground and could be trusted, Cheslaw explained. Hence, the cordial meeting.

Relieved that Cheslaw suspected nothing, Shaya remained on edge. He knew that the winking and gesturing only meant that the ruffians believed that Shaya could be more valuable to them without revealing his identity. The question was how. Shaya played out several scenarios in his mind. He could not afford to be naive as he was with his classmate. Suspect the worst of people, play out the possible responses, and hope for the best. That's how Shaya's survival instinct trained him to operate.

Author: Grandpa Shaya loved to play cards. He excelled at whatever games that involved using the hand you're dealt to outsmart opponents. No mercy during these games was allowed. It did not matter whether he was playing another elderly person at his senior living facility, his aide, or even his grandchildren or great-grandchildren. No throwing a game to a child to make them feel good. The only way to learn was to play – and lose. Use the hand you're dealt to succeed or not. And if not, try harder. Shaya reflexively calculated multiple permutations as games played out – possibly ingrained from his days in the forest, where his mind constantly raced to figure out how to react to all possible scenarios well before they happened.

One freezing evening, a few months after the chance meeting in the forest, the two familiar Russians and a third Russian, all armed with rifles and a belt with grenades, knocked on the Schwerdreskis' door as everyone was huddling around a wood-burning stove. They then burst in and demanded food. Mrs. Schwerdreski immediately scurried to comply as she gave orders to everyone to help out. Shaya peeled potatoes while the others prepared the meat and *kapusta* [cabbage] and set the table. All the while, the Russians sat near the stove, not saying a word but keeping a menacing eye on Shaya. After they ate and decided to leave, they asked Cheslaw to come outside with them. "Who is the guy helping out your mother?" the third Russian asked Cheslaw.

"We hired Geniek to help us out on the farm."

"Ask him to come out, we want to speak with him."

Cheslaw returned minutes later. "They want to speak with you, Geniek."

Running away was impossible. He was scared but had no other choice but to confront them.

"What do you want from my life?" he asked. "You want to kill me? Get it over with! Go ahead!" The Russians stood silently, looking at Shaya and then each other. They laughed at the temerity of this kid to challenge them like that.

"No, we're not here to kill you," one of the familiar Russians said. "However, you do need to get us bullets. Our sources tell us that Cheslaw has plenty of bullets around here. Find them and be ready next Monday at midnight."

"Or else..." barked the third Russian, intending to scare.

"Good night, see you on Monday," said the other two matter-of-factly. And with that, they left.

So much to process in so little time. What should he tell the Schwerdreskis waiting back inside? How could he get enough bullets without being detected? Would anything be enough for them?

"What did they want?" asked Cheslaw.

Quick on his feet, Shaya responded: "They asked me to join them, saying that I would not have to work as hard if I joined them."

Cheslaw and Mrs. Schwerdreski braced themselves, hoping Geniek was not about to tell them he was leaving. "I told them that you are good, kind people and that I am not overworked." Pleased with Geniek's loyalty and relieved that they would not be losing valuable help, the Schwerdreskis suspected nothing.

Finding bullets would not be hard. However, Shaya worried that Cheslaw might be keeping accurate records of his ammunition cache and feared getting caught. However, he feared the Russians more and had to risk it. He found closed boxes and open boxes. Figuring that removing bullets from the open boxes would be less detectable, he filled his pockets with bullets from the open boxes and waited for the

Russians the next Monday night. And the next. He got used to living even more precariously.

Within a few weeks, the Polish underground decided to switch gears. They had been largely successful in ridding the forest and random farms of Jews still in hiding, so they started to turn on the Russians who sporadically raided Polish homes. In early 1944, the Russians fought bloody battles with the Polish underground, with both sides suffering. Shaya tried his best to work like a horse for Mrs. Schwerdreski, hoping that neither Cheslaw nor his Russian nemeses would ask him to pick up a gun to join in the fighting.

One evening, the Russians came to Shaya's sleeping quarters with a wounded comrade. "Our friend Alex here was shot in battle; a doctor patched him up and prescribed some medication," one of them said. "He needs to rest for the next three days. And you are going to feed him, make sure that he takes his medicine, and rests here. We'll be back for him in three days." They helped Shaya take Alex to a secluded part of the barn and left.

Under unbelievable pressure, Shaya did the unbelievable – he tended to the needs of the wounded Russian soldier, did his normal chores for Mrs. Schwerdreski, and avoided detection – all on top of the baseline pressure of Shaya living as "Geniek" with antisemites to avoid detection. As he plowed through his days with gusto from one chore to the next, he wondered if his life would ever go back to normal. He thought he might be the only Jew left in Poland. He had no time to be sad about it, though, so he replayed his mother's words sporadically and busied himself full throttle with whatever he needed to do to stay alive.

Who Had it Worse?

Author: Papa Wimmer, who worked in multiple camps and had his whole family wiped out, told me several times: "Whatever I went through, your Grandpa Schloss had it much worse."

It was hard for me to fathom that Grandpa Shaya had it "worse" than his other grandfather, Romek. Yes, having to suddenly leave your family to run into the forest and never see them again was horrific. But the daily experience of slave labor, lineups, meager rations of food, and witnessing the constant brutality – how could Papa say that about Grandpa's experience? I couldn't wrap my teenage brain around Papa's calculus. While running through the Polish countryside posing as an orphaned Polish teen was by no means a walk in the park, Grandpa had pockets of time when he slept in a warm bed and had home-cooked food, albeit under a non-Jewish alias.

I thought about the stories I had heard from each of them. As a kid whose biggest discomfort was not being allowed to play his Atari video games for too long, it bothered me. It made no sense why Papa would say that Grandpa suffered worse. The teenage calculus went something like this:

They both lost their families and their homes. But Papa lost a bigger home. Papa was imprisoned, guarded by sadistic monsters, witnessed the murder of his rabbi and many others, and was forced to work 18 hours each day. Grandpa was on the run but never imprisoned. He had some rough stretches when he hid in freezing barns or thick forests, infested with lice, while living in constant fear of being detected by old schoolmates or anyone else who might detect he was Jewish. But Grandpa also had a few decent stretches when he worked on a farm and had three solid meals daily and a place to sleep.

The respective families' losses were a wash; the rest of the scale of misery seemed to tip Papa's way. It bothered me. Was Papa just being deferential to Grandpa? Perhaps because Grandpa was a year older? That's the best I could come up with, but that reasoning seemed way too superficial.

One Shabbos, Papa Wimmer told his family a story about a fellow slave laborer at Gross-Rosen who developed a huge abscess on his neck. The fellow hid it as best he could under his collar until the abscess grew so large that he couldn't turn his neck. This was a problem because often during roll call, the Nazis would order the prisoners to turn their heads. If anyone couldn't do exactly what was ordered, that could potentially be the poor laborer's last roll call. While all of the prisoners felt like they were living on borrowed time to a degree, everyone fastidiously tried to avoid giving the Nazis any excuse to be sadistic. The prisoner with the abscess fretted about it and seemed petrified.

Papa tried to brainstorm with others in the group, asking: "How can we help this guy? We have to help him! They'll kill him when they see he can't turn his head!"

Most were sympathetic but had no ideas. One frigid winter night after a snowstorm, Papa resolutely ordered no one in particular, "Go get me some snow and icicles!" Some icicles were hanging from the buildings around camp, and some of the prisoners dutifully gathered a few large ones from outside the barracks. Others filled some small buckets with packed snow. Romek sat with the fellow with the abscess. "Trust me," he said firmly as he asked others to hold the man down while he numbed the abscess and the surrounding area with snow and icicles. After a couple of minutes, Papa startled everyone as he pulled out a knife he had taken from the kitchen. The others thought he was crazy and might kill the guy. He immediately cut the abscess and drained out as much pus as possible as the man's scream pierced the night. The man eventually calmed down as his wound was wrapped with a makeshift bandage. Minor surgery complete. Thankfully, no Nazis heard the commotion, and the man lived.

As Papa told the story of the man with the abscess, Papa's gestures and retelling of the conversation made it look like he was describing events unfolding before his eyes in the present tense. I could not help wondering, "Okay, that's it, there's no way that Grandpa ever felt compelled to improvise surgery on anyone." Hands down, Papa's experience during World War II was way more horrific. The story, though, presented an opening for inquiry.

"Papa, you know how you've said that my other grandfather had to live through worse things than you did during the Holocaust?"

"Yes, of course, it was much worse for him."

The answer shocked me as Papa had just doubled down, even after that last story.

"Why do you say that? Actually, how can you say that?" With respectful teenage sincerity, I explained why it just didn't sound right. At best, they had different but equally awful experiences. But to say reflexively and unequivocally that Grandpa had it much worse appeared to be way overstated. What gives?

Without missing a beat, Papa explained: "Very simple. Your other grandfather had no way of knowing if he was the last Jew living in Europe. No one to confide in or rely upon while always having to worry about what might come around the next corner. To live through all that all alone must have been hell. In the camps, we at least had each other."

Liberation of Northeastern Poland

By April 1944, the Russian soldiers had stopped coming around. Perhaps they were killed by the Polish underground or the Germans. Shaya never found out. By the summer, the Germans were losing the war and the Polish underground had more or less stopped its activities due to the advancing Russian army. The Russians pushed the Germans out of Russia and were fighting on Polish soil. Sounds of heavy artillery punctuated the long summer days. The many hills and long valleys near the Schwerdreski farm made the area strategically valuable, so the Germans set up camp there to hold back the advancing Russians. For extra manpower, the Germans grabbed several Poles, including the Schwerdreskis'

"Geniek," to help dig trenches. Not long after the trenches were dug, bombs and artillery shells rained down. Shaya lay down and prayed. Ironically, he heard some Germans, whose only religion had been Hitler, call out to God for help too. When the shelling subsided, most of the German regiment was either dead or wounded. Others were walking around in shell shock. In broken German, he mustered the courage to ask a wounded German officer who had seen Shaya digging trenches before the shelling if he could leave.

"Yes," said the shaken officer quietly.

"*Danke shein* [Thank you]," said Shaya as he walked away through the field.

Another round of bombs and heavy artillery followed, and he again hit the ground. This time, when the shelling stopped, Shaya lifted his head and saw even fewer, if any, Germans who weren't wounded. "It was a miracle I was not killed then," recalled Shaya.

He returned to a festive meal at the Schwerdreskis'. Mrs. Schwerdreski prepared as much food as she could to celebrate the Russian troops' victory. Russian soldiers ate, drank, and were generally merry all over the property. One had a *balalaika* [ukulele] and led some rounds of Russian drinking songs. Shaya, though, couldn't eat or feel. He was numb and exhausted. Exhausted from digging trenches and years of hard farm work. Tired and traumatized from having to hide his identity.

The numbness was new, though, like an arm with the sensation of pins and needles as blood starts running through it again. His thoughts started to run beyond the daily grind. With the Germans defeated in this area of northeast Poland, he could start to strategize about life after the war. He thought about his brother Isaac who had been conscripted into the Russian army. Perhaps he had survived. Until Shaya could figure out a plan and no one tried to out him as a Jew, he saw no reason to give up the Geniek charade just yet.

Feigele Kamelgarn

Even though they were losing ground in the east to the Russians and fighting the Americans and British in the west, Nazi Germany decided to double down on the Final Solution – the systematic deportation, consignment to slave labor, and killing of whatever Jews they could still find. Feigele Kamelgarn (Shaya's future wife and my future Grandma) lived in the city of Lodz with her mother, brother, and sister at this point in the war; her father, Menachem Mendel Kamelgarn, had been taken to Siberia for forced labor and they had no idea if they would ever see him again. Stories of starvation and poverty in the Lodz ghetto are well-documented. Feigele never spoke about it, though. Around the same time that Shaya felt he could breathe somewhat due to the German retreat from northeastern Poland, Feigele's hell intensified as the Nazis decided to liquidate the Lodz ghetto and send Jews directly to Auschwitz.

Author: Grandma Feigele "Fay" Schloss may have been the most gentle person to walk the planet. She took simple but deep pleasure in being in the presence of family. She would bless us with "Everything you wish for yourself, Tatele." In the mid-1980s, Grandma and Grandpa moved to a two-bedroom condo in North Miami Beach. It was a tidy complex with many other Holocaust survivors nearby. Plenty of *lantzmen* [fellow Jews from the same region] to schmooze with and entertain. The community of survivors was something out of the movie Cocoon – people in their last healthy years enjoying the company of each other in their living rooms, dining rooms, clubhouse, pool, and shul.

Grandma and Grandpa had many friends there. Grandma's best friend in the Jade Winds Condominium complex was Feigele Binenstock. All of about four feet, ten inches, Feigele was a dynamo, full of energy. She walked five miles around the complex daily. The only thing faster than her gait was her sharp, feisty mind. Feigele and Grandma were also first cousins and survived Auschwitz together. It is hard enough to imagine going through Auschwitz; it is perhaps harder to imagine my gentle Grandma going through it without Feigele helping to pull her through.

Grandma was so delicate that I never mustered the audacity to ask her about Auschwitz. However, one time I do recall her volunteering information not long after the mystery of Josef Mengele's remains made the news in the mid-1980s. Mengele, the sadistic Nazi doctor who conducted cruel experiments on inmates at Auschwitz, had scurried to South America after the war along with other high-ranking Nazis. There were rumors he had drowned in Brazil.

The technology of the day ascertained that a certain body that had washed ashore was likely none other than the infamous Nazi doctor. There were reports about him and his probable death on the news and in magazines. Grandma watched a lot of news; it must have been difficult for her to hear his name even if he was now dead.

On hearing the news about Dr. Mengele, Grandma softly told us: "I met him." That was the first time anyone in my family learned anything about Grandma's time in Auschwitz, let alone that she had a brush with the "Angel of Death" on Earth himself. When she arrived at Auschwitz from Lodz with her mother and sister, Dr. Mengele efficiently greeted them as they stepped up to his table. A quick assessment of Grandma's mother, Breindel, and sister Leah followed. "Left!" he screamed at them. "Right!" he barked at Grandma. Grandma started to run to be with her dear mother and sister. Mengele stopped her and slapped her across the face. Hard. She touched her face as the blow still reverberated as she replayed the scene in her head before us. "And that was the last I saw them," Grandma said softly.

Grandma's tender nature was perhaps a coping mechanism. How can one better defeat the embodiment of evil, hate, and cruelty than to live a life of unpretentious kindness?

Other than her experience on arriving at Auschwitz and Feigele helping her pull through the toughest times, we know nothing of Grandma's experience at Auschwitz. Some things hurt too much.

The Angel

In a lesser-known story in the Book of Genesis, a nameless person referred to in the text only as "a man" appears and totally changes the course of Jewish history. Commentaries (Rashi) posit that the unidentified person was not a person at all; rather, the "man" was an angel on a mission from God sent to divert the course of events. While Romek Wimmer was fairly certain that the anonymous person in the following story was indeed human, he was also certain that the trajectory of his entire life was dramatically impacted by this godly person – a man whose name he could not recall or perhaps ever knew.

After liberation, Papa and his colleagues stayed in the camp in Langenbielau. Following years of back breaking work, the elation of newfound freedom was muted because now, for the first time, Papa and his friends in camp had time to contemplate the gravity of everyone's losses and had to make choices about where to go next. Newly free people would post notes in public areas:

> "Looking for family members _____;
>
> last seen in _____."

Most people never found their relatives. Despondency prevailed.

One evening, a week or two after being liberated, an American rabbi came to his camp. In Yiddish, he announced to everyone but to no one in particular: "*Minyan* tomorrow morning. Come to minyan tomorrow morning!" He was trying to round up people for morning prayers, which required a minyan, the requisite quorum of ten. Papa saw this guy and was incredulous and frustrated. Minyan? Is he serious? Does he not know what we just went through? The 22-year-old approached the rabbi with youthful defiance. It was a Friday evening and Shabbos was about to start.

"I just went through years of hell," Romek said. "I lost my whole family. My parents. My brothers. My sister. Friends. My rabbi – it happened in front of my face, right after Yom Kippur! Romek's volume increased as he continued to challenge the patient American Rabbi.

"Minyan? Are you kidding me? How dare you tell us or even ask us to go to minyan?! What's the point? Don't bother us with your minyan." Others watched as Romek spoke for the group. "We don't believe in God anymore. Why should we? Where was He?"

The rabbi patiently listened as Romek vented with a barrage of defiant questions. The rabbi had no answers. Romek and the others knew he would have no concrete answers. The young men did not expect what happened next.

"Would you rather have been killed?" asked the rabbi. "You instinctively prayed for this day to be able to live your life again. Now that it's here, you have choices to make. Stay where they forced you, or live again in your family's memory in spite of those who put you here?"

For the first time in years, Romek had the chance to reflect on things larger than just getting through the day. And at this point, Romek still did not anticipate any day involving minyan.

The rabbi listened to Romek's pained grievances without interruption but did not back down. He stayed up with Papa late into the evening, giving an ear and giving comfort. When Romek had said all that could be said, the rabbi hugged him.

"My dear fellow," the rabbi said softly, "if you don't come to minyan tomorrow, they win. You can't let that happen. You went to minyan before. You need to come again now that you can. You and your friends went through horrible things; your family was murdered and…"

"And the *rav* [rabbinic leader] of my town, Rabbi Frenkel, right in front of me!" Romek again interjected to accentuate his point about prayer being pointless. "It didn't help him."

"And we can never forget that," replied the American rabbi, "but now is your chance to start your life again. After a *churban* [utter desolation], you have to rebuild. That's what we Jews do. You are young and have to focus on the future. You and your friends have to find Jewish women, get married, and start Jewish families. Every Jewish family is another proof that they did not and cannot win. The road to rebuilding starts with minyan tomorrow. It's part of your parents' legacy. They made sure you know how to daven, so daven you must. Say Kaddish, yes, of course. Mourn. But you also have to daven for your future and the future of *Klal Yisrael* [the Jewish People]."

Years of slavery had made it difficult to think about serving God in any capacity. Though Romek still knew how to daven, doing so was the last thing on his mind. Amid the cruel drudgery of the munition factory and the work camp, all mental energies were naturally focused on getting through the next day or week. This heart-to-heart talk with the American Rabbi in the *mamaloshen* [mother tongue] of Yiddish was the first time in years that Romek had the opportunity to reflect on his loss in the context of focusing on the long-term. It was a shiva visit of sorts: the rabbi comforted Papa for his losses and encouraged him to live purposefully as his family once did.

The kind rabbi's words resonated deeply and touched a raw nerve. Romek and his friends joined the rabbi at the minyan on Shabbos.

Romek Wimmer (1945)

Before sunrise on Sunday, the rabbi gave Romek a pair of *tefillin* [leather straps connected to a box that contains scripture] to use at minyan the next day. Tefillin are worn on the arm, with the scripture boxes facing the heart, and on the head. They are meant to remind their wearer to use their heart and head in loving and serving God. While Romek did not dive into minyan head or heart first, he resolutely decided to attend minyan the next morning; that's what his parents and rabbi would have wanted. From his bar mitzvah until the Nazis forced Romek out of his home in Wieliczka, Romek had worn tefillin each weekday. Davening with tefillin for the first time in years that morning brought back memories of when he first put them on in Rabbi Frenkel's shul as his father proudly helped the excited 13-year-old adjust the straps just so – not too tight to cut off circulation, not too loose to unravel.

As Romek concluded his davening, he sadly wrapped up the tefillin and approached the American rabbi to return them. But the rabbi would not accept them back. "You wear these daily," he said. "I know you will." And he did.

The nighttime talk and the gift of the tefillin galvanized Romek to live a life steeped in the tradition of his parents. He donned them every day (until he upgraded to a nicer pair years later) just as he had done before the war. Romek attended minyan and wore tefillin each weekday for the rest of his life.

Author: We still have that set of tefillin. It is a family treasure.

Papa Wimmer proudly purchased tefillin for his son, grandsons, and his oldest great-grandson. His second great-grandson became a bar mitzvah shortly after Papa died and proudly wears Papa's tefillin daily.

Papa's encounter with the American rabbi was no less impactful than Jacob's encounter with an unnamed "angel." Both "chance" meetings changed the trajectories of generations.

Liberation for Sala

In the months leading up to May 8, 1945, the ladies in Sala's camp, Langenbielau, could sense that change was coming. The German SS women were less nasty and even let hints of current events seep through their usual snarls. "You must be happy that the Russians are near, right?" they snapped a few times. On May 8, 1945, the Russians came, told the prisoners they were free, and opened the gates that surrounded the barracks.

Some of the girls had brothers in the camp next door and were able to reunite. Most did not have such luck in reuniting with relatives. En masse, the prisoners from Langenbielau's men's and women's camps decided to go to the next closest town, Reichenbach, approximately five km (three miles) away. The Reichenbach townsfolk fled when the Russians liberated the camps; they were afraid that the Jews would start rampaging through their town once liberated. The now-former slaves found empty homes in Reichenbach. The young men kicked in locked doors and took over abandoned homes. Sala and five others stayed at one house; six others stayed next door. The whole town that had been free of Jews was quickly full of now-free Jews.

Finally, with time to think about their relatives, they started wandering the common areas and posting notes to try to find them. That's how Sala found out that her brother Isaac was alive. Isaac survived Buchenwald, a death camp. When the Americans came to liberate Buchenwald, they saw dead people all over. In the days before Buchenwald was liberated, Isaac and a friend contracted typhus. The two of them were left for dead in the middle of a pile of corpses. When the American GIs came to Buchenwald, they screamed, "You are liberated! You are liberated!" Those lucky and capable enough to remain standing were elated. Isaac and his friend, both barely alive, mustered whatever strength they still had to start moving, and a GI noticed that one of the death piles appeared to be in motion. Isaac and his friend were living skeletons – dry bones coming back to life – and were taken to a field hospital. There, the Americans fed people little by little to avoid overwhelming undernourished bellies, nursing them back to health. (Neither knew what became of the other until decades later when a rabbi in Boynton Beach, Florida, who had heard both of their stories, randomly and separately, reconnected them.)

The young men and women started meeting each other. Shlemek "Sam" Poznanski, who was with Romek in camp, met Sala and was immediately smitten. Sam was a friendly, jovial young man despite the hardships he had just endured. Like most of his fellow survivors, he had lost his family. Sam set eyes on Sala, a spunky Jewish girl from a similar background, and tried his best to woo her. Though flattering, Sala's mind was elsewhere; she wanted to find her brother and aunt

Esther. She knew that her parents and sister had been taken to a death camp yet held out hope that she might find her brother and aunt. Sam was relentless, but Sala was adamant. "No," she said.

"Sala, you have to think about who you will marry," Sam said. "Why not me?"

"No. Again, for the thousandth time, no."

Sam saw he was getting nowhere but made one last pitch, "Okay, I'm not for you," he said. "I get it. But you have to meet my friend Romek. He's such a mensch. You'll love him."

Romek was not just a friend. He and Sam became brothers and saved each other's lives by having each other's backs countless times. Sala sensed the sincerity and said, "Okay, I'll meet him."

Sala Dreksler, 1945

Shaya Still in Danger

With no more German soldiers threatening the area, the Russian soldiers filled a vacuum. "We liberated you, you should be grateful to us, we'll therefore take what we want" became the prevalent attitude of the Russians who remained in the area where Shaya still masqueraded as Geniek. Most of the locals were indeed grateful and showered their Russian liberators with adoration and gifts. That was not always enough, though.

One day, a Russian captain and some subordinates looking for additional manpower came to the Schwerdreski farm as Shaya and Cheslaw were working. They asked a few questions and demanded that Shaya join them. "But I have to finish my work!" he protested.

"No, you don't; you come with us now," they replied. And with that, the Russians forced Shaya into the back of their vehicle.

"If you're going to kill me, just get it over with!" he said.

That was not their intention. Instead, he was taken to a regiment that was backing up Russia's front-line fighters. As the Russians kept advancing westward, so did this unit about five to ten miles behind, providing logistical support. After some initial questioning, they conscripted Shaya to assist in the kitchen. He did so for a few weeks, and when he noticed they had stopped watching him too closely, he bolted. He ran for hours – again, on the run through an unfamiliar and unforgiving Polish countryside. Shaya hoped that he could somehow find someone, anyone, who had survived to help plot out his next steps.

It was not to be. A truck with two Russian soldiers from the camp he had just deserted found him wandering on a road. "How did you get so far so fast?" they asked. They seemed more intrigued than perturbed, even a bit sympathetic.

Shaya could not hold it in anymore, so he unloaded his real story on them. "And after going through hell from the Germans and Poles, I just don't have the strength to go through another hell with you people," Shaya said. "You didn't even let me bring a sweater or change of clothes from the farm I was at. I told you everything I know and you just keep holding me for no reason. Let me be!"

They smiled and even seemed to agree with the justness of Shaya's request. "But we have orders, sorry," they said, and back to camp they went for Shaya to face some more questioning by a senior officer.

The senior officer treated Shaya respectfully, offering him tea and a cigarette. Though it was hard to see who else was in the kerosene-lamp-lit room, Shaya recognized the voice of one of his favorite Russian soldiers – one of the two who had sporadically forced Shaya to steal bullets from Cheslaw Schwerdreski and other mischief. Shaya's mind raced again. *What could they possibly want now?* he wondered.

The next morning, they placed Shaya on the back of a truck, drove a few hours, and opened up the back.

"You can go," they said.

"But where am I?" he asked.

"Been that long, huh?"

Before they drove away, they laughed that Shaya did not immediately recognize they had taken him back to his hometown of Ostrów.

Once Shaya had his bearings, he gravitated toward the direction of his parents' house, unsure and a bit scared of whom or what he might find.

What Next?

With no families to go back to, Sala Drexler's friend Machusha came up with a brilliant idea for them and their other friend, Balcza, to support themselves. They all were now expert seamstresses. Before the war, Machusha had left a large, brand-new sewing machine with a neighbor.

"Please watch it for me until I return," Machusha had said.

"Of course," said the Polish neighbor.

They'd get the machine back from the neighbor and open up a shop somewhere. The three young ladies figured they would remain a while trying to find relatives who might also be gravitating back toward their homes. With the bonus of picking up the sewing machine, they'd support themselves for a while.

When they arrived in town, they noticed no Jews around, only glaring stares. Undeterred, they naively knocked on the door at Mechusha's neighbor's house, hoping to retrieve the sewing machine.

"You're alive!" the neighbor screamed in shock and horror as if she had seen three menacing zombies instead of three determined orphans looking for the slightest kindness.

Mechusha only wanted to reclaim one item. And then would have happily left. However, before Mechusha could ask for her machine back, the neighbor menacingly said, "Leave now!" making it clear she preferred they would have been killed with most of the town's other Jews. The young ladies were shocked that the previously kind neighbor would act this way. They ran out of town as fast as they could without the sewing machine, happy to get away with their lives.

Shaya after the war (1945)

A House, But No Longer Home

When Shaya reached his family's house, he found that one of his parents' competitors had moved in. They had taken over the grocery business and now the house, too. He caught the new owner off guard and alone when Shaya came to the door. The Pole was surprised and seemed nervous. Shaya had gone through enough at that point to understand the futility of demanding back his parents' house and chose to extract information instead. Shaya put his parents' competitor at ease: "I don't want anything back," he said. "I just want to know if you heard of any other Jews surviving."

He curtly told Shaya of one Jew who he heard was in town and shut the door. Shaya knew the family that the man spoke of but did not find any other Jews in Ostrów.

Shaya played back the last few years in his head, before living as Geniek at the Schwerdreskis, and tried to retrace his steps to see if any of his cousins or friends had survived.

He remembered his cousin Goldy and her husband, Efraim Epstein – the ones whose baby was accidentally smothered as they tried to evade capture – who were hiding along with another cousin, Shmulke Mishler, at the Pastors.

Shaya was confident that the Pastors were good people. When he got to their farm they greeted him warmly and told him what happened to his cousins. First, they confirmed that Shaya had made the right call to move on; not long after Goldy asked Shaya to stay with them, the Pastors simply could not support them and hide them safely. Instead, the three cousins had to move around and sporadically visited the Pastors, who gave them food before they went back on their way.

In the last few weeks before the Russians pushed the Germans out, Goldy, Efraim, and Shmulke were hiding in a large wheat field. Some Poles found them and reported them to the Germans, who did the dirty work of killing Goldy and Efraim. Shmulke managed to run away, but without his cousins, he was like a lost sheep. Numb from losing his companions, he stopped thinking rationally. He managed to live through the next couple of weeks wandering around a bit, with the Pastors offering food when he came by.

Shmulke then took a rifle from the Pastors and marched himself to the Pasrtelewiec family home. The Pasrtelewiecs were rabid antisemites who Shmulke knew took items from his parents' home. He also suspected they were involved in reporting Goldy and Efraim to the German authorities to curry favor. When Shmulke came with his rifle, he knocked on the door and demanded his parents' valuables back. Mr. Pasrtelewiec invited him in and went to the next room where his two daughters were messing around with their boyfriends. Even though he was armed, the boyfriends overpowered Shmulke, dragged him outside and killed him with his own gun. The Pastors found out from the two hoodlums, who bragged about it.

Survivors Regrouping

Shaya spent the next weeks desperately trying to connect with someone, anyone he knew. It had been years since he could confide or rely on another Jew and he missed his family dearly. Eventually, a trickle of Jews who had survived either in camps or in hiding made their way toward the area of Ostrów. Shaya chanced upon two pale, thin boys from the Huss family. They recognized Shaya immediately and begged him not to go. They, too, were excited to see someone they knew from before the war. Their parents were friends with Shaya's, and their warm greeting uplifted Shaya with a taste of family. "Our parents just went out to get some food, they'll be back soon," they said. "Please stay until they come." Miraculously, the Huss family survived due to the largesse of a Polish farmer who hid them successfully. They were one of the very few Jewish families that remained intact.

"Shaya, we're going back to Ostrów," Mr. Huss said. "I spoke to the family that lived in our house. Come with us."

"I was there a few weeks ago," Shaya responded. "Are you sure you know it's safe?"

Mr. Huss was a resourceful fellow, not naive. Around the time Shaya went to Ostrów, some local Poles couldn't stomach Jews returning there and started killing Jews again. However, the Russians wanted to maintain order and did not want the violence to spill over. Mr. Huss learned that the Russians would be patrolling and allowed Jews to carry guns to defend themselves. As survivors from nearby towns started to trickle back only to find less-than-welcoming environs, and as word got out that it was safer in Ostrów, the town became the gathering place for Jews of that area to regroup.

With each survivor who came to Ostrów, Shaya found purpose again. He learned their stories of survival and shared his own. Most were not as physically able as he was, so he helped wherever he could. Within the relative safety of Ostrów and a burgeoning social network, Shaya found himself a bicycle and ways to make money. He bought and sold jewelry and foreign currency.

One heartbroken woman originally from Lodz, named Janina, had evaded capture by hiding in the forest and living with a kind Polish farmer with her eight-year-old son, Wacus. The Germans killed her husband and the rest of her family. She made her way to Ostrów from the Polish farm where she was staying to find other Jews. After miraculously surviving, a Russian truck accidentally ran Wacus over. Wacus was now recuperating in a Russian army hospital with two broken legs. Shaya was moved by Janina's story and helped bring food and other items of comfort to Wacus, who was released from the hospital a few days later. As part of his regular rounds of checking in on survivors who needed help, Shaya rode his bike one town away from Ostrów, where Janina and Wacus were staying.

In February 1945, the Russians liberated Lodz. "Shaya, I need to see if it's safe to go back to Lodz," Janina said. "It's a bigger city than Ostrów. It's probably going to have the same protections in place. If any of my extended family survived, I need to be there. Can you keep an eye on Wacus for me?"

Shaya gladly found himself able and willing to be responsible for the well-being of someone other than himself for the first time in years.

"Thank you, Shaya," she said. "I'll be back as soon as I can."

Lodz was about 225 kilometers (140 miles) southwest of Ostrów. It took Janina about two months to return. She found a relative, Ruzia, who had taken over another relative's apartment with her husband, Levi. From the time she arrived in Lodz until she left, the Jewish population increased from a few hundred to a few thousand. Much like the Jews of Shaya's area of northeastern Poland who gravitated toward Ostrów, Jews from all over Poland were finding each other in the central Polish city of Lodz, except on a greater scale. "Shaya, you'll find more opportunities there," she said. "Please come, or at least please visit us!"

Shaya was hesitant to leave northeastern Poland as he still hoped to receive information from the Russian authorities about his brother Isaac. So he stayed with the Huss family and spent his days peddling and helping out other survivors as best he could. After a few months of receiving no definitive word on Isaac, Shaya was told that Isaac had been fighting in a unit that took heavy casualties, but he received no definitive word on whether his brother made it out alive. After months of waiting, Shaya understood he could no longer credibly believe that he would ever see his brother, the last holdout of hope to regroup with his family.

Shaya longed for connection. Some of his relatives – an uncle on his father's side and an aunt on his mother's side – had left Poland for the United States just as things were turning ugly for Europe's Jews in the 1930s. As Shaya was deciding whether to stay with the Husses or move to Lodz, a mail carrier came to Ostrów and approached Shaya.

"Maybe you can help me," he said. "I have a letter from New York in the United States addressed to a family I can't find." He allowed Shaya to open the letter. He knew the family and asked the mailman for a few minutes to write back:

I have been in Ostrów for a few weeks now since liberation; I know your family, but unfortunately, I have not seen any of them return to Ostrów yet. Hopefully, they will. If I see them, I will tell them to write to you. If you could please do me a favor, please try to contact my uncle Abraham Schloss and my aunt Sosha Mishler to tell them that their nephew Shaya Schloss survived. Thank you, Shaya Schloss.

Sure enough, the letter made its way back to New York and the recipient placed an ad in the Forward, the Yiddish newspaper that all Jewish immigrants read. Shaya waited about a month to see if any of his American relatives might try reaching him if they knew for certain he had survived. Almost a year later, he learned that Aunt Sosha, an avid Forward reader, saw the ad.

Author: After liberation from Auschwitz, my Grandma Feigele Kamelgarn returned to her Aunt Ruzia and Uncle Levi's apartment (Aunt Ruzia was a successful businesswoman and lived in a luxury apartment before the war), hoping to find it in family hands. (Levi was Feigele's uncle – her father's brother). When she came to the apartment, Feigele met her Aunt Ruzia's cousin, Janina, who was living there with her son, Wacus, and her new husband.

House Foregone, but Not Forgotten in a COVID-19 Bar Mitzvah Speech

Romek heard what was happening to some Jews who had returned to their homes only to find uninvited caretakers having moved in with no intention of ever leaving. Though some cordially refused to leave, others resorted to violence to discourage the Jews, who were not expected to survive, from reclaiming their properties. Romek knew that his family's six-family house in the central town square of Wieliczka would be a prime target for takeover. He inquired about his house but did not push it. Romek expected that Polish neighbors would have moved in. Years later, he learned something unexpected.

Author: It has long been a tradition for a young man coming of age as a bar mitzvah in the Orthodox world to "give over a p'shetl" – to elucidate to the crowd of well-wishers about a topic of either the oral law or the Torah portion of the week. The biblical passages of Joseph and his brothers are well-known. The twists and turns of Joseph's fate – his brothers appear to dash his dreams of grandeur by throwing him into a pit, only for him to experience a slow and steady rise to power in Egypt under an assumed name – have enthralled both casual biblical readers and serious Torah scholars. My nephew, Jonah Schloss, was fortunate enough to have the latter part of Joseph's story in his *Parsha* [Torah portion], when Joseph unmasks his façade of being a maniacal despot out to cruelly keep Benjamin as punishment for a trumped-up charge of royal theft. Jonah was fortunate because the story is so compelling.

Jonah's bar mitzvah was celebrated on a Thursday morning in 2020 with few people physically present with him in the synagogue but approximately 150 people spanning the globe and several US states dialing in via Zoom. They all watched Jonah read a portion of the Torah with perfect cantillation and heard him relate a compelling story found in his Parsha to an amazing story about his great-grandfather, Papa Wimmer.

Jonah observed that all siblings quarrel sometimes; it's a given rite of passage for virtually anyone with a brother or sister. However, try to imagine being thrown into a pit by your siblings, then being sold by them to merchants, and then lying to your parents about it and keeping it a secret. Most people, even those blessed with extreme patience, would likely feel no moral compunction to show those siblings compassion when given the opportunity to turn the tables. Yet that is exactly what Joseph did. As the Egyptian viceroy, second in power only to Pharaoh, Joseph had the opportunity to exact revenge on his brothers who sold him off 22 years earlier. These same brothers came to Egypt to bring food back to Canaan. Joseph did not hold a grudge and longed to see his aging father. Yet Joseph understood that if he were to reveal himself to his brothers immediately, they would always have in the back of their minds the idea that, "Well, he's being nice to us now because he wants to see Dad; we still have to watch our backs."

So Joseph concocted a scenario where the brothers faced déjà vu. If given the opportunity to save themselves by ignoring the plight of the only surviving son of Rachel (Benjamin), would they do it? Or would they challenge the viceroy and stand in unity with their brother?

Joseph overheard the brothers express remorse over how they had treated Joseph, and Judah chose to confront the Egyptian viceroy. At that point, Joseph revealed himself and comforted his brothers, expressing that God Himself had sent him to Egypt. No vengeful outburst, just a genuine loving reunion among brothers who had all suffered ordeals.

Joseph's story reminded Jonah of a story he had heard about Papa Wimmer and the six-family home designed by his grandfather that overlooks the town square to this day.

Apparently, a cousin who knew Papa had survived got to the home first after the war, filed some papers claiming to be the sole heir, and sold it sometime in the late 1940s. The cousin moved to Israel shortly thereafter.

On Papa's first visit to Israel, in 1964, he located that cousin. The cousin owned a small jewelry store. Papa put on a pair of sunglasses and covered his eyes with the brim of his hat as he entered the store. "May I help you, sir?" the cousin asked.

Slowly, Papa lifted his hat and removed the sunglasses without saying a word. When Papa told me the story, he would laugh and chortle: "He thought I was going to kill him. He turned so white like he saw a ghost!" Papa did no such thing. He took no vengeance or recompense. He accepted God's plan as it played out.

Yes, Papa relished the drama. But he also relished the big picture of being in Israel with a relative – albeit one who sold his family's home – as part of that plan. Only a short few years before the reunion in the jewelry store, Papa and this cousin were going through the hell of Nazi persecution not knowing what the next day would bring. The thought of Jews reuniting in Israel? A fantasy. Though Papa had a legitimate gripe with his cousin, in the scheme of Jewish history, why spoil a dream come true with a quibble over real estate? No one would have believed such a meeting could have happened in the early 1940s.

Jonah's recounting of this story in the context of Joseph triggered several tears among the Zoom and live audience spanning Israel, Canada, and the US. The bigger picture, of course, was that Papa's great-grandson was attuned enough to compare Papa to the biblical Joseph.

Moving on from Lodz to Föhrenwald

Shaya made the trek to Lodz to find more survivors. After years of being alone, he enjoyed the company of other Jews, all of whom had lived through their own hells. When he met people, he asked about their stories and compared notes.

Fay and Sam Schloss, Lodz, 1945

He did not initially think he had much in common with Janina's cousin, Feigele Kamelgarn. She was from a big city, he knew his way around farms. He was outgoing, she was more reserved. She was refined, he was a coarse country bumpkin. Though the losses of Shaya's entire family and Feigele's mother and sister loomed large,

Shaya and Feigele spent about three months dating and focusing on life moving forward. Her Aunt Ruzia and Uncle Levy Dzialoszynski (pronounced Jelloshinski) gave them a push to marry. Levy, Feigele's mother's brother, counseled the young couple not to wait. He said Feigele's father, Mendel, who was making his way home from Siberia, would surely understand the young couple starting their lives together. So they did on October 21, 1945.

Even though survivors were making their way to Lodz, most soon realized there was no viable future there. It was merely a waystation before moving on to safer places. The Russians fancied themselves as entitled liberators and were making Jews' lives uncomfortable. Word got around that the American zone in post war Europe was safer and would allow people to better plan their next steps. So, a week after Shaya and Feigele married, they made their way with whatever small belongings they had to the Föhrenwald displaced persons camp in the American zone in Munich, Germany.

They traveled from Poland through Czechoslovakia, Austria, and then to Munich by train with Feigele's brother, Murray (Moniek), and another recently married couple, Jezek and Dorka Birenz. They encountered several Russian soldiers on the trains who, once they realized that there were some Jews on the train, copped the attitude that had prompted them to leave Lodz: "Aren't you grateful that we liberated you? Don't you think you owe us?" The two young couples were fortunate to get off the trains with whatever the Russians had not already taken from them.

When they finally got to Föhrenwald, they found Shaya's cousin, Shmulke Goldberg (the only other living member of the family photo in 1935), his wife, Esther, and their newborn daughter living there. (Shmulke's wild story of survival, including being one of the few to have escaped from Treblinka and living in a pit in the forest for over a year, was chronicled by his daughter-in-law, Karen Treiger, in a book titled *My Soul is Filled with Joy: A Holocaust Story*.)

Shaya and Feigele were given one room to share with Feigele's brother, Murray, and two other Jewish men. Crowded and unpleasant by any standard, it was very uncomfortable for the new couple. They lived off rations provided by the United Nations Relief and Rehabilitation Administration (UNRRA), the UN's refugee organization at the time.

For some in Föhrenwald, though, UNRRA rations didn't cut it. M any of Shaya and Feigele's peers bought and sold what they could on the black market. Shaya wanted to continue this way since he had done so in Ostrów before coming to Lodz. But Feigele worried about the trouble Shaya might bring them if he were ever caught. No longer on his own with only himself to rely upon or make a decision, Shaya safely deferred to his wife and they lived within their means. For the first time in a long time, the stakes of Shaya's options were not exactly life or death.

Would he have preferred to *mach gesheft* [make business] and try his hand at the black market? Probably. But he was comfortable relying on whatever meager provisions they had. In any event, as cramped as they may have been, it was several steps above sleeping in freezing barns infested with vermin and other unfriendly places not knowing what to expect the next day. The decision not to engage in the black market represented a shift in thinking. No longer did they have to wonder where they would have to flee next. They could opt for the safest choices. Above all, he was grateful to finally have someone else's well-being to consider. They had each survived years of high-risk situations. In their new life together, they decided to minimize risk whenever they could.

By May 1946, a letter from Shaya's Aunt Sosha in New York, who had seen the ad in the Forward, reached him in Föhrenwald. Someone from Ostrów forwarded a letter to Lodz. The letter made its way to Uncle Levy and Aunt Ruzia, who then sent it to Föhrenwald. Furthermore, Feigele's father finally came back from Siberia and made his way to Föhrenwald to reunite with his daughter, son, and new son-in-law. It was a bittersweet reunion given the loss of his wife Breindel and daughter Lea, yet they realized that life must and does continue, even after horrific tragedy.

When Feigele and Shaya's son was born in August 1946, they tied small red strings on his wrist – a superstition to ward off the *ayin hora* [evil eye]. They took no chances, physically or spiritually. They named him Jacob, for Shaya's dear father.

A Fast Postwar Courtship

Romek Wimmer became a bit of a wheeler-dealer after the war. He worked the black market selling anything he could get his hands on – cigarettes, sugar, butter. Staples sold. It was risky, but most of his friends were doing it, and whatever risk he was taking paled in comparison to working as forced labor for the Nazis.

One day, Sam Poznanski told him, "Romek, you have to meet this girl; she's got so much *chein* [charm], like you. "Considering that Sam and Romek would not have survived without having each other's backs in camp, Romek needed no further references. For their first date, Romek finagled a motorcycle and invited Sala Drexler to hop aboard.

Romek charmingly rode up to pick up his friend Sam's acquaintance, young Sala Drexler. "She was so proper and polite – and clean," Papa recalled with a chuckle. "And then we went for a ride, zzzik! We went so fast and then right into a puddle! She got so dirty, and I couldn't stop laughing." Sala was so good-natured about it and Romek so affable. It was hard to resist another date after that.

From that day on, Sala stayed close to Romek, eventually becoming the most affable, loving foil a man could hope for.

Left to right: Irving Drexler (Sally's brother), Sally and Jack Wimmer on their wedding day, April 1946

'Whistle!'

Author: Papa Romek was always playful. Especially with his dear "Kotush" (Polish for "kitten," I believe), my Nana. When Papa called her Kotush, he was usually engaging in a friendly cat-and-mouse game. My dear Nana watched what Papa ate like a hawk. She knew what foods were good for him and those he should be avoiding (or at least eating in moderation). She knew it better than he did. Of course, he appreciated that his dear wife cared so much about his health. Nonetheless, he would often sneak another piece of kugel or an extra piece of chocolate by his loving gatekeeper. There was probably one thing he enjoyed more than actually eating any forbidden food. It was the sport of trying to sneak it past Nana.

At a Shabbos meal, for instance, in the middle of the meal, the conversation would predictably go something like this when Nana left the table to busy herself in the kitchen:

First, he would create the diversion. "Hey, Nana," he called to her playfully and indignantly, using the title Nana to imply that their grandson deserved some dessert that she was unjustifiably withholding. "Don't you have something, *eppes* [Yiddish for "something" – saying it twice in different languages for emphasis] for dessert? Some cooked apples, a piece of chocolate? Something? Nothing? *Nu* [Yiddish for so], what's going on here?"

With a silent "I know exactly what you're trying to do, so don't even think of it" nod, Nana would take a step back from the kitchen, glance back to the dining room and retreat to the kitchen.

"Hey, Jona!" With a quick whisper and a pleading wink, Papa sought to recruit a co-conspirator. He didn't think it prudent to use all three syllables in my name, Jonathan, lest he be caught by taking the additional time to utter three syllables.

He would then point to the corner kugel piece that was a bit well done, the salt, another piece of challah, a morsel of chocolate, or a small cookie. Next, with childlike raised eyebrows and a stifled giggle, his index finger would beckon for it in quick desperation. The grandkids had seen this play out so many times and could never resist Papa's predictably adorable overtures. About half of the time, the food smuggling missions successfully ended with an "atta boy" wink as Nana returned to the table. Inevitably, sometime later that night, Nana would say things to me like, "You think I don't know that Papa adds more salt when I'm not looking? I made the recipe with just a little less so he would feel extra good, like he was winning something, when he decided to add more salt without me looking."

The other half of the time, he got busted in the act. Big time. Inevitably, it went down like this:

Just after he put the treasured morsel to his taste buds, Nana would sternly, yet wistfully, call out from the kitchen, "Romek, whistle!" By calling him by the name his fellow campmates used, she was alluding to a less idyllic episode from their past lives. During the long pause between Nana calling him Romek and the crescendo command to "whistle" while eating forbidden fruit (or, more likely, cake or kugel), I could see the myriad of emotions embedded in this game.

First, he knew he was busted. Badly. So he started to try to keep himself from laughing. If you're chewing, it is nearly impossible to whistle. Trying to suppress laughter, chew, and whistle at the same time is physically impossible.

Nonetheless, the chocolate was already his to savor at that point; he had sneaked it by the guard (to a certain degree). So while he was chewing, he'd gesticulate to me to help him out with a whistle. But I couldn't whistle the way he could. His laughter was compounded by my pathetic attempt. He'd also laugh because he thought he was the victor in this little game – and he was.

But not over Nana. The irony of the "whistle" challenge was that these two love birds didn't make it up. Years earlier, while performing slave labor for the Nazis in a kitchen, the sadistic Nazi officers required Jewish workers to whistle while they worked to prevent hungry kitchen workers from sneaking bites of food intended for Nazi brass. While Romek was largely successful in sneaking food past his tormentors, he could rarely, if ever, sneak anything past his beloved Salush.

By surviving and thriving with a loving spouse and their grandchildren, the laughter was indeed a laugh of victory.

Counting Cookies

Author: The Schloss grandparents had a different culinary competition of sorts. Grandma and Grandpa each made their own signature sugar cookie. You had to eat the same amount of each kind because they kept score of whose batch was better received. If he saw Grandma's cookies disappearing faster than his cookies, we'd hear it. "Maybe you'd like this better, Tatele," Grandpa would half ask, half cajole as he pushed a small cardboard box closer to us. Grandma wouldn't say a word but clearly enjoyed having the favored cookie, quietly giggling as she shrugged her shoulders with each muffled chuckle. In retrospect, each cookie mirrored the personality of its baker. With Grandma's cookie, you could bet on how it would taste just by looking at it. Perfectly round with a sun-like color and a slight flakiness around the edges, the sugar cookie would melt in your mouth – a culinary delight from start to finish. Grandpa's cookies had a rough texture, a pale alien-like color, were shaped like a horseshoe, and did not immediately melt on the palate – the crushed almonds he diced in there did not lend themselves to that. But, boy, was it tasty! One can't judge a cookie, or a person, by the exterior. Both can be a bit rough around the edges and in different ways, but there is so much to savor.

Making a Living

Romek relished the give and take of the black market. Anything that could be sold was fair game and he relished the excitement. However, Sala preferred that Romek pursue something more stable. She tolerated it for a while and encouraged him to slow down his activities. Indeed, thanks to Romek's parents who set him up to intern with Dr. Schlang as a dental assistant in Wieliczka to stay out of trouble, Romek had a practical foundation.

In 1946, Romek found a way to make money besides the black market. Building on the training he had earlier received under Dr. Schlang, he enrolled in a dental training program in the American zone of post war Germany. Tinkering with teeth and dental molds became a lifelong passion not just because it provided a livelihood. It also reminded him of where he came from. His parents appreciated his skills and passions and cared to set him on the path back in Wieliczka; he would not let them down.

While he attended the program to become a certified dentist, he still spent some time at the black market – trading items like cigarettes for butter or other useful items. Resources were scarce and there was a market for anything people could get their hands on. Papa constantly worked hard to trade up for things that could help provide for his family. While Papa reveled in the free market (and even managed to procure a motorcycle), Nana came to dislike the potential dangers of working the black market.

With a baby girl at home and young wife, Sala believed it more prudent to focus more on Romek's passion for dentistry. Of course, she was right. Though the rush from black market dealings may have been fun, he, with some encouragement from Sala, realized that those dealings, like a sugar high, were not necessarily healthy or sustainable – so he dabbled in it but did not spend full days on it.

Papa's passion for dentistry wouldn't wait for certification. Unlike when he declared himself to be an engineer to make it past a selection, he actually had dental experience. Now in his mid-twenties, he yearned to find the opportunity to pick up where he was abruptly interrupted by the war. He looked around Munich for a dentist to mentor him. A fellow survivor who was also liberated in Langenbielau, Srulik Frank, introduced Papa to a German dentist. Though the dentist was likely a Nazi, Papa didn't care about his prejudices as the man was an excellent technician willing to accept some help. In the years after the war, Papa did business with anyone he could. He was not shy or lazy about his goals. He wanted to support a young family and act on his passion for dentistry – preferably doing both at the same time while giving 100 percent of his efforts to both his family and his trade.

In the months following the war, they needed a place to live. With assistance from the Americans, some Jews lived in apartments formerly occupied by Nazis. Papa went to the Joint Jewish Distribution Committee in Munich in December 1945 for their help. With their assistance, he, Nana, Nana's brother Irving, and Nana's aunt Esther moved into a small house at 575 Lerchenauer Street. A Nazi named Wartush lived with his wife and daughter in the attic upstairs. Mr. Wartush spent most days smoking his pipe and reclusively staying up there. Mrs. Wartush and their daughter became friendly with the patrolling American soldiers and acted pleasantly enough with the young survivors living downstairs. When the Wimmers' daughter Betty was born, Mrs. Wartush and her daughter even played with her. Many Germans wanted to be friendly at this point, whether out of fear of retribution, guilt, or something else. Those that couldn't stomach it, like Mr. Wartush, stayed to themselves. It was hard not to get along with Papa, though. He did business with whomever he could.

Whether it was a former Nazi dentist or Germans in the black market, Papa valued people for what they were at the time he was dealing with them and did not probe their past potential misdeeds. "We were forced. What could we do?" was the prevailing apologetic attitude in Munich. The German dentist immediately could tell that Papa had some valuable training that could benefit his practice, so he gave him work as a dental technician. As with Dr. Schlang, Papa had the opportunity to observe the dentist pull teeth and perform root canals. Papa would perform actual dental work before he was certified.

Jewish Backbone

In May 1948, Romek, Sala, and their friends were glued to their radios. When the United Nations voted in favor of recognizing the State of Israel, they saw it as a miracle. The Soviet Union and the United States both voted in favor! Just as the Cold War was beginning, the world's two superpowers actually agreed on something. Asked about it years later, Romek said, "We thought it was a miracle. We thought that this was our reward, our compensation for what we lost – our parents, our families – to get a State of Israel that our parents did not live to see, but we have survived. And lived to see the rebirth of the State of Israel." For millennia, Jews all over the world had been praying three times daily

– "our eyes look for the return to *tziyon* [Zion] with mercy" and "to Jerusalem Your city, may we return with mercy." Until then, those prayers were uttered wistfully, a pleading, perhaps with a sigh in the face of years of violent antisemitism geared to crush Jews and their spirit of hope. With the UN vote, Romek felt God had miraculously intervened to give Jews all over a backbone and help them stand proud unapologetically.

American Charity

After years of waiting and letter-writing to Shaya's American relatives, Shaya, Feigele, their son Jacob, and Feigele's father Menachem Mendel Kamelgarn and brother Murray all received papers from sponsors to emigrate to the United States. Rumors were flying around Föhrenwald about immigration protocols on arrival. Was Jacob too young? They did not want to get turned back after weeks of travel over a technicality, so they listed his birth date safely within whatever few-month window was deemed an acceptable age for a child to emigrate to the United States. In May 1949, Shaya, Feigele, and Jacob crossed the Atlantic on the Marine Jumper. When they got off the boat, Uncle Arnold, Aunt Mollie, and several cousins greeted them warmly and took them to an apartment they had rented for them on Tiffany Street in the Bronx. They had stocked the apartment with pots, pans, dishes, and towels. Describing what Uncle Arnold, Aunt Molly, and crew set up as charitable understates the tremendous kindness done. More than benefactors, they provided the solace and practical support of a genuine family. Jacob and Feigele were each diagnosed with the mumps a day after arrival, so they did not stay at the apartment until they were both cured. They stayed at Uncle Arnold and Aunt Molly's place a few blocks away as she tended to them as she would her own sick children.

While greatly appreciative of the largesse, Shaya did not want to remain a burden. He needed a job. The first job he found was at a nonunion dress shop that paid 65 cents an hour – a full ten cents below minimum wage. Though he remembered how much he hated interning for a tailor with his friend Mordechai Zolzberg in Ostrów, Shaya jumped at the opportunity to support his family. He was the only Jew on the hot, stuffy floor and he still hated the tediousness of working with clothes. Nonetheless, he rolled up his sleeves to make a go of it.

Uncle Arnold noticed Shaya's zeal but saw how visibly miserable the young man was when he came home from work. Arnold owned a painting contractor business and had already hired Feigele's brother, Murray. But Shaya was determined to make it on his own, doing what he could to support his family. Until he wasn't. After three months in the dress shop, Shaya took Arnold up on an offer to work as a painter. It was harder physically than working at the dress shop, but Shaya tolerated the work better than he did sitting at a table with fabric. Uncle Arnold's union shop paid $90 for a 35-hour work week for a full painter's wage.

It took Shaya three years to hone his skills to reach the level of full painter. Along the way, his peers noted how skilled a painter Shaya had become. He received several offers from peers to open their own painting business together. Shaya contemplated it more than once, but he could not leave Arnold on the spot; he owed him too much. It was worth a conversation, though. When Shaya told Arnold about how he had been approached, Arnold discouraged him. "People who have a steady job shouldn't look for *glicken* [luck]," Arnold said. He urged Shaya to play it safe. Did Arnold discourage Shaya because he valued him as a prized workhorse for his company, or was Arnold concerned that Shaya might fail as an entrepreneur? Probably a little bit of both, but the safer, and therefore the default choice, was to stay put.

Certificate of Professional Status as a Dentist - US
Zone of Germany (1949)

A Postwar Dental Practice!

In July 1949, Papa became a member of the Jewish Dental Association in the American zone of Germany. In August 1949, he received the official certification he needed to be able to treat dental patients from the International Refugee Organization under his own shingle. His patients had horrible teeth as most were survivors who, for years, had no access to dental care or means to practice oral hygiene.

With the Certificate of Professional Status, Papa was able to set up shop. Ever the deal maker, Papa arranged for the German government to pay for treating his patients. As long as a survivor had papers documenting their refugee status, Papa was able to treat them without charge. Many survivors took the opportunity to visit Dr. Wimmer's office on Germany's dime. Papa even took an ad out in the local Jewish newspaper in Munich. It read: "*Jydishe* [Jewish] Dentist. Bring Your Documents. Closed on Shabbos." In 1951, papers to come to America finally came through. Though he would not be able to practice dentistry in America, there was no future in Germany. The long boat ride on the General Blatchford induced nausea for most on board.

While Papa was seasick for most of the trip, Nana looked after Betty, who entertained those around her by dancing and singing. Betty's energy was a sweet reminder of the hope they all shared. Though the journey was long and arduous, the new life these refugees hoped to forge in the United States held tremendous promise.

They settled in Brooklyn on Starr Street with whatever they could carry, including their boisterous little girl. Never afraid of working hard, Papa and Nana each worked quickly to learn English. Some fellow survivors helped him find work delivering sandwiches to sailors on the ships docked in New York Harbor on the Hudson River along the West Side Highway. Papa's charm and exuberance endeared him to the sailors, who tipped him well. After putting in a day's work selling sandwiches, Papa would go to English class. Betty motivated him. "I love to play with my daughter," read one of his practice notebooks for writing. He peppered his notebook with other such endearing gems.

Though always willing to do whatever it took to put food on the table, he did not want to give up dentistry. Even though he was still in his twenties, he had spent almost ten years dedicated to the field – first as an apprentice at 14 in Wieliczka (until a rudely-forced hiatus), picking it up again in Munich as a student and intern and then as a full-fledged dentist servicing survivors.

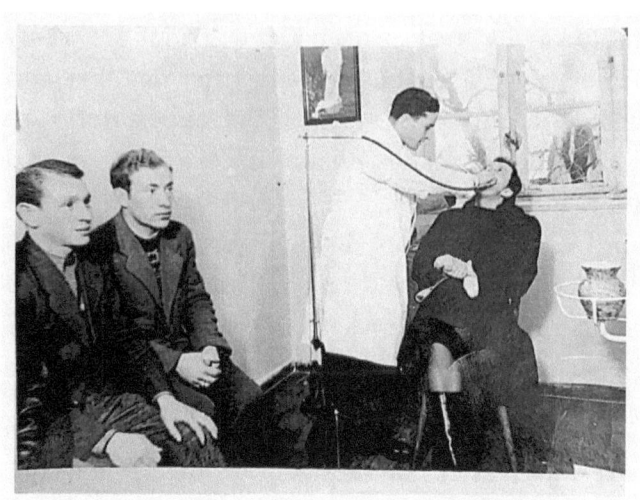

Servicing other survivors in Germany, 1949

Actual dental drill used by Jack Wimmer in Germany (same device as in black and white photo, above), now a conversation piece in Sally Wimmer's living room, 2024.

Dentistry, 1960s

Papa Wimmer, by then called "Jack", found work in a dental lab working on porcelain teeth. He was a bit of a perfectionist when it came to his work and took tremendous pride in it. He would painstakingly make sure that the shade of white or off-white matched perfectly. His boss appreciated the work ethic and, of course, the work itself.

Papa never obtained a license to practice dentistry in the US, but he had a passion for all things teeth. First of all, teeth make great business; everyone is a potential customer. (Everyone has teeth, right?). In his career in the US, Papa found a job in a laboratory making models of teeth. Papa did great work and was extremely reliable. Few if any of the technicians who worked in the dental lab were also certified dentists like Papa. At lunchtime, Papa would sometimes venture outside with his food and sit on a park bench near their office at 30 Central Park South with other technicians.

They often talked about how they really could do the same work for themselves, but for most of them, it was just talk. For Papa, who could not afford to take the time to recertify in the US, the ticket to remain in the business of teeth could be opening up his own lab. When he decided to do so, his boss made an enticing offer. He offered to pay for a down payment on a house (up to $5,000) to encourage him to stay. That was big money. But not big enough for Papa to take the entrepreneurial leap to risk working for himself. As a nod to the humble park bench from which the idea for this career pivot emerged, Papa named his dental lab "Park Dental Studios."

Park Dental Studios was hopping with activity. It attracted excellent dental technicians. In the late 1950s and 1960s, it was on the cutting edge of a burgeoning new sub-specialty in the field of dentistry – dental implants. Even more than the high level of work that was performed daily, what made his company tick was that its employees were treated like family and were extremely loyal in return.

In 1966, tenants were being encouraged to leave their building at 9 West 57th Street. Plans to demolish it and erect a skyscraper were underway. As leases came up, they were not renewed. Those with leases with years left on them received offers to leave. Papa "Jack" Wimmer was approached by certain building managers with an offer. "Please take this generous offer to leave, Jack," he was not-so-subtly nudged. "Why should I go?" he asked naively. "I have a lease! What can they do?" Well, nothing. Legally, that is.

One morning, when Jack came to the office, the place was a wreck. Tubes of materials had been squirted out all over the floor. Desks and chairs were overturned. Papers were thrown about. Pieces of equipment were missing or broken. The message had been sent: "Operate your lab elsewhere or just try to operate a dental lab here." The choice was painfully obvious. Suddenly, listening to the building managers' offer didn't seem too bad.

Park Dental Studios moved across the street from the Empire State Building at 19 West 34th Street. The dental laboratory, which had a couple of dozen employees at the time, far exceeded expectations. At its peak, Park Dental Studios had almost 30 employees who were treated like family.

Unique Tenancy

Jack Wimmer sold Park Dental Studios to a large corporation in 1977. He then pivoted to operating as a dental implant wholesaler and rebranded as Park Dental Research Corp. In 2011, Wimmer sold Park Dental Research Corp. to Dr. Ronald Bulard of Oklahoma. From 1966 through 2018 (yes, even after Jack's death in 2017), Park Dental resided at 19 West 34th Street.

In the early 1980s, 19 West 34th Street's new owners wasted no time in making noticeable renovations. The updates and upgrades to the elevators, hallways, and bathrooms all gave the old office building sitting in the shadows of the most famous building in the world a new look and feel.

When the Domanskys' PDR Realty bought the site, Park Dental was about six years into a ten-year lease. Not long after PDR Realty spruced up their new acquisition, Papa called the new landlords to set up a face-to-face meeting.

"What does he want?" Mr. Domansky asked his son. Mr. Domansky himself was a survivor who had built a mini real estate empire. The second generation was establishing itself in the business.

"He probably wants to renegotiate his lease, like everyone else," said the junior Domansky to his father.

The father-son team of landlords agreed to meet their tenant.

At precisely the scheduled meeting time, Papa knocked on his landlords' door. Dressed in a sharp suit with a red power tie and small fedora, he was ushered into the Domanskys' office.

After initial pleasantries, Papa got down to business. "I see what you've done to this building," Papa said. "You've made it nice and I appreciate that. I would like to pay you more in rent so you should keep up the good work." Two jaws hit the ground. Never in their decades-long history of being landlords in New York City, nor any time since, had any tenant made such a pitch. They were impressed with this sincere businessman. Park Dental stayed on as a tenant for several more decades. The building was always in first-class shape, and they treated this first-class tenant in kind.

For the last decade of its tenancy or so, Park Dental had no written lease – just a handshake agreement to pay as long as the business needed and wanted space in the building.

Apprenticeship in a Hot July

Every day, Shaya "Sam" Schloss trekked from the Bronx all over the city, taking multiple trains and buses. He painted at some of the city's most prominent buildings – the World Trade Center, the Waldorf, you name it. When the job demanded top quality, Sam was the man. With his all-day physical labor, Shaya did not need to work out. He was an ox of a man in his prime.

Shaya would come home exhausted and full of paint. Feigele always had delicious food ready for him in their immaculately kept apartment when he came home. But before they sat down to eat, Shaya would wash up and Feigele would lovingly help him peel whatever color of the day's paint job was off his arms, neck, and face, counting the days together until the union pension would kick in at 62 and Shaya would finally be able to take things a little easier.

Their oldest son, Jacob (now Jack), saw his father, his uncle, and a cousin all in the painting business and just assumed he'd get there, too. As a young teen, Jack begged his father to take him on a job to get a running start on the family trade. Shaya put him off. After all, Shaya's father, Jack's namesake, was a cerebral person. He loved books, sang, and played a musical instrument. Shaya had long resigned himself to having to make his living doing physical things; that was his lot in life and was content with it. But his son? An American with a great public school education? He wanted something better for Jack.

But the lad persisted. "Okay, let's go," Shaya said to Jack one hot summer day in July. Jack eagerly rode the subway to Manhattan, excited to work among men with his dad as the foreman. When they arrived at a building under construction, Shaya showed Jack how to stroke paint properly. *I can do this!* thought Jack. They then proceeded to an apartment on a high floor with no windows, fans, or air conditioning.

"You start in here, then make your way to the living room," Shaya said, leading Jack to a closet that was more like a sauna. Before he even picked up a brush, Jack's sweat started to flow freely. "Don't come out until you finish," Shaya instructed. In later decades, child labor laws may have technically protected Jack from having to paint that closet and living room under those conditions. But Shaya had made his point without actually having to say anything to discourage Jack from following in his footsteps. Jack never asked to come on another painting job (and eventually became a lawyer).

Wall of Fame

Watching Papa Jack Wimmer prepare before going on a trip to lecture about implants was like watching an elite athlete go over game film to prepare for the next game. His big leather satchel with the slide projector and the slides arranged perfectly looked impressive and important. He would go over his points with a pointer and then pack everything up neatly. Papa had a unique perspective on both the history and practice of dental implantology.

He met, became close friends with, and worked with the pioneers and legends in the field of dental implantology. Papa was one of the few people in the field to have real, hands-on clinical experience and also an understanding of how to make and what goes into the dental devices that have become so common nowadays.

As a kid, I would hear about "Lenny," Dr. Leonard Linkow, as though Papa were talking about his favorite schoolmate. Lenny was known as one of the most influential pioneers in the field of dental implantology. I didn't fully appreciate Lenny until I had to do a "visual speech" for speech class as an undergraduate student. The assignment was to give a five- to seven-minute speech that involved a visual aid. Papa's slides seemed primed for the task. I called Papa to ask if I could borrow the projector and some slides. "Of course!" He was thrilled that I showed some interest in his work. "You come to my office; I'll show you everything, my dear grandson!"

With Papa's office directly across from the Empire State Building, it was a bit of an adventure. The hustle and bustle of the area in the shadow of New York's iconic edifice fed into a certain energy that permeated Papa's third-floor office. The office had a small reception area with a long hallway leading to Papa's desk and a conference table. Along the hallway wall was a dental Wall of Fame of sorts. It was filled with plaques and framed certificates for lecturing at dental conventions all over the world and with photos of famous dentists. Not quite a trip to Cooperstown, but I understood his enthusiasm – these dentists were legends and the places he went to lecture about implants (always with Nana) were varied and impressive – Australia, Belgium, China, Iran, Israel, Italy, Mexico, Spain, Switzerland, and all over the United States – to name some. Not bad for an immigrant who came to the US without knowing English.

Photos of Dr. Linkow, Dr. Isaiah Lew, Dr. Charles Babbush, and others who are widely known as the fathers of dental implantology also adorned the wall. Their works are studied in dental schools. Papa explained who each of those dentists was with the same enthusiasm and awesome respect that an older baseball fan would explain a Hall of Fame baseball player's exploits to a young fan. To the uninitiated, it may seem dull, but it certainly captivated those who follow. Papa not only followed these dentists, but he played on the same proverbial field with many of them just as dental implants were becoming popular.

The other parts of the office were primarily areas where orders were taken and processed. Papa also reserved a small room for himself to "tinker" – a small welding area where he would manipulate metals. Sometimes he would fix or adjust some dental widgets. It was also a play area of sorts. I have a pair of cufflinks he made there, for instance.

After Papa's tour of the Wall of Fame, he showed me some old implant models and explained that they were among the first dental implant prototypes. Some of the molds used for implants on monkeys were in a glass cabinet along with what seemed an endless array of small metal implants. Look magazine featured some of Park Dental's products in the early 1970 s as being on the cutting edge of dental technology. A framed cover of the edition was proudly hung behind the conference table. A large sterilization chamber stood across from Papa's desk. It was used to sterilize certain blades before shipping.

Papa gave me the long tour, which included his catalog. Each of the old molds and models had a story. I adored Papa, but after a while, I got so bored.

At first glance, it looked a bit like the chambers in Superman's Fortress of Solitude, I remember thinking. On one level, it was hard to stay interested. On another, I was witnessing a master artisan talk about his craft. He gave this same tour to top dentists from all around the world when they made the trek to New York – and now, he was giving me the same red-carpet treatment. It took a bit for that to sink in, and I felt privileged and proud.

"Subperiosteal dental implants are placed under the gum, but on or above the jawbone; this type of implant is useful to patients who do not have enough healthy natural jawbone and cannot, or do not want to, undergo a procedure to rebuild the jawbone," Papa explained. He authored chapters for implant textbooks and wrote articles on implants and dental laboratory technology for dental periodicals. This was his passion. And it certainly came across that way. While some of the gory slides seemed to go over well with some of my peers, I doubt that I conveyed even one percent of his enthusiasm in my speech.

Many of the items on Papa's guided tour of his office eventually did get enshrined in a museum. Not in Baseball's Hall of Fame, but in a Museum of Medicine in Venice, Italy.

Successful Fishing Expedition
Staten Island, NY 1969

Nana and Papa had a summer home near the water in Staten Island. Though technically in New York City, the Staten Island home offered a quieter pace and more bucolic life than their attached two-family home in the middle of the Bronx. Not long after my parents Jack Schloss and Betty Wimmer married in June 1969, Nana and Papa invited the *machatonim* [in-laws] and the new couple for a late-summer Sunday afternoon. Eager to impress his cool new brother-in-law, Howie Wimmer, his wife's little brother, suggested they go fishing a few blocks away. Not one to say no, Jack agreed to take Howie but politely asked Papa and Grandpa Sam to come along, too.

"No, thank you," Papa answered. "You go, we stay here. Bring back some good fish!"

Off went the new brothers-in-law for a bonding experience. The experience was memorable but had nothing to do with catching fish. In fact, Howie and Jack, both novice fishermen, did not catch anything. The weather wasn't great. They probably did not thread the bait properly, or perhaps they just went to a bum spot on the dock. While Jack and Howie went off, Papa and Grandpa talked and bonded over their shared experiences from the old country. Then Papa decided to have some fun at his son's and son-in-law's expense. He and Grandpa went for a walk along the docks, came across a fisherman with a bucket full of fish, and decided to buy the entire bucket.

As the hapless young fisherman returned from their hours-long, lackluster adventure, Papa and Grandpa showed them the bucket.

"How many did you get?" they asked. "We got so many!" Jack and Howie just looked at each other incredulously as Papa and Grandpa laughed at them playfully.

"We didn't get any! Where did you go?"

"Oh, we must have been upstream from you and caught them all before they got to you."

I think that's when Howie decided to take up golf.

"Good Morning, Jack Wimmer Here. We Need a Minyan." (Fort Lee, NJ, 1989)

Papa Wimmer loved going to shul daily and involved himself in daily operations on all levels. Some background – in Orthodox Jewish circles, a minyan of ten males over the age of 13 is needed to say certain prayers. Among them, most famously perhaps, is the Kaddish prayer, which mourners recite for departed close relatives within the year of death and on the anniversary of the death each year. Even less affiliated Jews often see it as a solemn duty to attend synagogue to say Kaddish for a loved one with a minyan.

When Jack and Sally Wimmer's daughter and son-in-law went on a short vacation to visit the Schloss machatonim in Florida for a few days, their teenage grandson (me) stayed with them. One rainy Tuesday morning, nine males over 13 showed up, one of whom came to say Kaddish. Papa felt obligated to help and relished the opportunity to have his grandson witness him in action just a few minutes after *shachris* [the morning prayers] had started. No one else could have pulled this off. Papa winked at his grandson, gesturing to follow him to the phone in the kitchen.

"You watch," he said with an impish wink as he picked up the phone to dial.

"Good morning. This is Jack Wimmer," he said with all the confidence as if a CEO were speaking to another CEO.

Groggily, quizzically, and apologetically, a woman's voice on the other end says, "It's 6:34 in the morning, Jack."

With resolute urgency, he persisted, "I'm sorry to wake you, but we need your husband for a minyan. Someone is saying Kaddish and we only have nine."

"But he's sleeping."

"You get him up now. Please. We need him."

She clearly sensed the broad, confident smile on the other end of the phone. "Hold on, Jack."

As the phone went silent on the other end, Papa gave me a wink of confidence that he had just closed the deal, although he was holding the phone between his ear and shoulder while flipping through the shul directory in case he needed to make another call.

After a brief pause: "He'll be there in five minutes."

With another wink, he summoned me over. "You see that?" he asked with self-satisfaction but without an ounce of bragging. In addition to making the minyan, it was a teaching moment for his grandson. "You have to push sometimes and not be afraid to take action."

A Horrible Job

For some winter breaks, we visited Grandma and Grandpa Schloss in Florida. Their condominium complex was something like the senior complex from the movie *Cocoon*. A gated community with palm trees, a clubhouse, pools, nice landscaping – an overall private and tranquil feeling pervaded. They bonded with the many other survivors who found solace there and loved to show us off to their friends, especially in shul. They *kvelled* [were bursting with pride] that their grandchildren who came to visit from New York could proficiently participate in, and even lead, services. They would introduce us to their friends, who would then excitedly exchange some Yiddish with my grandparents while pointing, patting, hugging, or kissing me on the cheek as they spoke. It felt awkward being a showpiece, but even as a teen, I understood it to be therapeutic for them in a way. It gave them such a boost.

After services one Shabbos, I was in the crowded shul hallway and accidentally brushed up against an elderly man's arm from behind. Before I could politely apologize, he yelled at me in Yiddish as if I had done something horrible. It was strange and a bit out of character for this crowd of kind survivors. Of course, I apologized profusely even though the man's reaction was wholly disproportionate to what I had done. Hearing the ruckus, Grandpa came over and pulled me aside, and I explained what had transpired. Grandpa sighed. "You should excuse him, Tatele," he said, pausing and sighing again before continuing. "He had a horrible job during the war. The Nazis made him stay by the ovens, putting dead people in and cleaning up ashes. His nerves are shot. He gets startled very easy. Don't be offended." I wasn't and shrugged off the overreaction.

The Yeshiva Phone Call

In 1992, I spent a semester abroad at a Jerusalem yeshiva that catered to American yeshiva high school graduates. Two pay phones serviced the entire campus. With snail mail to and from the US taking about two weeks, the opportunity to speak on the phone was a rare prize. When one of the phones rang, anyone would pick up and race to locate the intended call recipient. A call from America always added a level of urgency. As I was sitting in class one afternoon, I heard my name being called in the hallways: "Jon Schloss! Some guy Jack Wimmer is on the phone for you!" I jumped out of my seat, ran to the pay phone, and grabbed the dangling receiver. I don't remember what he said, but I do remember what the rabbi whose class I had abruptly left said to me when I got back. I was fully expecting some griping about running out too loudly. Instead, the rabbi seemed uncharacteristically awestruck by my presence in class.

"You know Jack Wimmer?" he asked.

"Of course. He's my grandfather."

"Wow. Do you have any idea what a *tzadik* [pious person] he is?"

I did, but did not know the connection between this American-born young rabbi in Israel and my grandfather in New Jersey. "How do you know him?" I asked.

"My father worked at Park Dental Studios for many years. Your grandfather is a fantastic boss and a very generous man."

Throughout the rest of the semester, the rabbi seemed overly appreciative that he had the opportunity to teach Jack Wimmer's grandson. I did not pry or fully understand why at the time.

Years later, I had a similar interaction that shed some light on the 1992 interaction. In 2019, about two years after Papa died, I met an elderly man and his daughter at a shiva house (a "shiva house" is a home where close relatives of a deceased receive consoling visitors for seven days after burial). We were sitting next to each other in a packed living room as we waited for our turn to console the mourner. The daughter quietly struck up polite conversation. She introduced me to her elderly father, a retired dental technician.

"My grandfather was in that biz for many years, too," I said. "He passed away a couple of years ago."

"Oh yeah? What was his name?"

"Jack Wimmer."

It was as if I had uttered the Divine Name. The woman seemed awestruck and became slightly teary-eyed. "Your grandfather was Jack Wimmer?"

"Yes."

She gently elbowed her father to get his attention.

"My father here worked for Jack Wimmer at Park Dental Studios dental lab for 11 years. We are able to afford our standard of living today for my dad because of what your grandfather negotiated on his behalf when he sold Park Dental Studios. We know that he didn't have to do that." The woman was the rabbi's sister.

Apparently, Papa made sure that his employees were cared for. We had no idea that whatever deal he struck when selling Park Dental Studios in 1977 continued to impact his employees as late as 2019.

Walk Out if it Does Not Make Sense

Papa entertained several offers for his lab before selling it in 1977. One was for a sum that seemed almost too good to be true. Papa hired a large law firm to help him evaluate the deal. They did their due diligence and said he had a legitimate offer from a savvy buyer in hand.

"We've ironed out some language and they're ready to sign, Mr. Wimmer; the offer is indeed good." Papa went to the firm's office, still skeptical but open to hearing more. He was invited into a beautiful conference room where the potential buyer and their lawyers were sitting with Papa's lawyer in front of a stack of documents. The lawyers on both sides had clearly negotiated such deals before, probably with each other. The sale of Park Dental Studios would soon be another accolade on these lawyers' mantles. Papa asked that the proposed deal be explained slowly, in English, not legalese.

After listening intently, Papa fully understood. For a pittance of a down payment, Papa would retain a minority share. The balance of the purchase price would be paid over several years, contingent on sales. This company knew little about dental labs but a lot about milking cash cows. That did not sit well with Papa. He knew every aspect of the business and sensed nothing from anyone in the room to inspire confidence. These buyers could easily run the company into the ground before they would have to pay.

"So you'll be paying me with my own money and you're guaranteeing nothing?!" Papa asked in disgust to all present, to no one in particular. No one answered or made eye contact as his words hung in the air. His spot-on analysis left no doubt. Eager for a deal to advertise their prowess, his own legal team had urged him to sign on the dotted line without fully explaining the transaction.

Papa had cut through the pretension with that one astute observation. Pleas from his law firm that the purchaser was safe to deal with fell on deaf ears. Papa walked out with his head held high. He did not appreciate the "talk, talk, talk" of the large-firm lawyers.

"These guys, they talk so much and say nothing," Papa later told me. "I walked out, and they were all shocked I did so. But what do I care? I'm the only one still sitting with any risk. You can't just look at the price. You think I should have signed just because they printed all those papers for me to sign? Sometimes you just walk away – what will they do to me?" he asked, shrugging his shoulders with an impish grin.

When it came to business (and, to Papa, just about everything was "business"), action spoke much louder than words.

"Make Fish!"

Starting in my college years, Papa sporadically called me with a message that to anyone else would seem strange, almost clandestine. I wish I had saved at least one of the recordings on my answering machine: "Hey, Jona, it's Papa. I need you to make fish. Call me back," he said, with the emphasis on the importance that fish be made. Quickly. He wasn't asking me to try my hand at baking him the latest catch, especially considering my limited culinary skills. He needed me to write a concise letter to someone with a specific, urgent message. I was not the only one to get these calls. My uncle, father, mother, and brother also had to make Papa "fish" at times. I'm not sure how Papa divided the labor.

Why was "fish" the code name for succinct writing? It has to do with the story that Papa loved about the fishmonger with a marketing dilemma.

A young and eager fishmonger opened a fish store. Excited to advertise his fish, he made a big sign with huge letters and hung it prominently in front of his store: "FRESH FISH SOLD HERE." The fishmonger's friends came to congratulate their friend on the grand opening. The first friend came to the store.

"Who would sell rancid fish?" the friend asked rhetorically. "By saying 'fresh' on your sign, it looks like you're probably covering up the rotten fish. Of course, your fish is fresh. You don't need to advertise that."

Good idea, thought the fishmonger. So he changed the sign. It now read: "FISH SOLD HERE."

The next friend came and said to the fishmonger, "You're not selling over there," the friend said, pointing down the block. "Of course, you're selling fish here. You don't need 'here' in your sign."

Good idea, thought the fishmonger. So he changed the sign again. He proudly put up the new sign, which read "FISH SOLD."

A third friend came and wondered aloud: "Are you giving away your fish? Of course, you're selling fish."

"Good point," the fishmonger said. "It's a good thing I'm in the fish business and not the advertising business." Thanks to the help of his friends, the newly business-savvy fishmonger needed only one word to market his offerings: "FISH."

The "fish" I made for Papa over the years included letters to dentists, dignitaries, friends, condo boards, and rabbis. He always had a message that he wanted to get across without wasting too much time or ink. After I became a lawyer, contracts were added to the list of the types of "fish" I made for Papa.

"My Lawyer"

While Papa's alacrity served him well over the years, his inherent default toward haste sometimes had less-than-stellar outcomes. Case in point: traffic tickets.

While I never handle matters in Family Court, one of the running jokes in the family is that I do, however, practice "family law" (with a lowercase f). My first such client called me less than a year after I was admitted to practice law in 1999.

"Hey, Jona, I need a lawyer."

"Why, Papa? What did you do?"

"How do you know I did something?"

"I just figured you did something."

Papa then irately explained the situation between giggles. "I've been driving on this street for many years now," he said. "I make a right turn and the cop pulls me over and gives me a ticket."

The nerve.

"So why did he give you a ticket?" I asked.

"I need a lawyer to fight this. I do this all the time. For years, no ticket. Now, a ticket. It is not right," he said with impish yet truthful indignation. I knew there had to be more to the story.

"You know why you got this ticket?!" I heard Nana ask in the background with the intonation and implication of both the prosecuting attorney and sentencing judge.

"Jona, you see how much I need a lawyer," he said as he broke out into laughter. "Even Nana won't defend me."

"Well, I was just admitted," I said. "I don't really know much about traffic law."

Trying to get out of it was useless.

"You a lawyer or what?" he asked. "What's going on with you? I need a lawyer. You are a lawyer, and I need one. You come with me to court."

Hard to argue with that logic.

So I read up on pleading down moving violations. I also eventually got the full story. They did change the traffic pattern – where he used to be able to turn right on red legally, there was now a clear "No Right on Red" sign. Right turns at that red light had been illegal for about two years. Nonetheless, over Nana's objection, he had continued making the turn the entire time. She not-so-secretly rooted for him to get a ticket to teach him a lesson. Now he needed a lawyer.

When we checked into the local justice court, the court clerk perfunctorily read off the list of people there for traffic tickets.

About half the people had attorneys with them. The unrepresented on the list responded "Present," while those with lawyers responded: "Present with counsel."

"John Doe?"

"Present."

"Jane Smith?"

"Present with counsel."

As the clerk made her way down the alphabet, Papa started to smirk and fidget anxiously as she got closer to the Ws.

"Joachim Wimmer?" the clerk called.

"I am present, with my lawyer, who is my grandson!" Papa proudly exclaimed to the packed (and, until now, very bored) courtroom.

The judge even looked up from his papers. "Interesting, never heard that one before," he said.

I was able to plead down the ticket to a nonmoving violation. The judge told Papa that I did a good job. Papa readily paid the ticket and was happy that he technically got away with making a right on red, which Nana had repeatedly told him not to do.

Filling Needs without Fanfare

Before the Nazis came to town, Papa's family was fairly prominent. Not only had Papa's grandfather, Solomon, designed their six-family home, but his father, Nachum, was in charge of the local marketplace, which was just steps away from their home. On Monday and Thursday, farmers and artisans would sell their wares in the Wieliczka market, each setting up shop in a booth. Nachum arranged the booths and charged the sellers for them. One such booth was run by a farmer who brought chickens.

After the war, Papa naturally gravitated toward other survivors, one of whom was from Wieliczka and had also made it to America with a wife and child. The survivor was a few years older than Papa and had a story about how his family never lacked for chicken on Shabbos, even if they didn't have enough money that week, because Papa's mother always made sure to send enough chicken for the family. His mother provided chicken not only for this survivor's family, but also several others, the man said. She did it with no fanfare. She just saw a need and filled it. (I don't think that my cousin Rebecca knows this story about our great-grandmother.

Nonetheless, Rebecca started "Feed-A-Family" – a grass-roots food bank in Modi'in, Israel, geared toward helping families that have fallen on tough times.)

A few months after Papa died in 2017, a member of his community told us a story we did not know but did not surprise us. The community member was active in a charitable organization that helps absorb new immigrants to Israel from around the globe. There was a young woman immigrant from Ethiopia whose teeth had been knocked out. The injury was particularly demoralizing for this young woman of marriageable age. She simply wanted a "normal" smile again.

A local dentist had offered to help her by waiving his fee for doing the necessary dental work to place the implants that would restore her smile, but the dentist did not have any extra implants to use. Papa donated a full set of them through the organization for the woman's procedure, along with the most cutting-edge equipment to ensure a healthy and speedy recovery. The young woman can now confidently speak and smile without feeling self-conscious.

There was a need. Papa felt privileged to be able to fill it and did it without fanfare.

The Wedding Album

Mostly, the grandkids saw the laughter and fun. My grandparents masked the pain unnecessarily well. They had every right to behave bitterly, yet when the "old country" came up in conversation, the memories were uniformly pleasant. Benevolent parents, playful and mischievous or studious siblings – the sunnier memories of normal family life before World War II largely outshone the dark times in camps and ghettos.

Of course, I always knew that each of my grandparents had lost most, if not all, of their families in the Holocaust. I had it all documented on my chart from fourth grade, after all. But the gravity of those tragedies became palpable at unexpected times.

For instance, the first few pages of my wedding album have photos of my beautiful bride and her immediate family, followed by photos of me and my immediate family. Next are photos of the new couple and their extended families. I have two pages of extended family photos. My wife, a fourth-generation American whose lineal lines were not ravaged on all sides by World War II Europe, has quite a few more.

My grandparents, all beaming in every photo, cherished each wedding and other milestones, seeing them as another victory for those who value life over those who worship death and destruction. Even as a young adult, it didn't occur to me until I saw my wedding album how small my family was and how large it could have been.

The Israel Day Parade

Every June, there is a large parade along Fifth Avenue in Manhattan held to show solidarity with the State of Israel. Schools, synagogues, bands, non- profits, and private companies from all over march in colorful T-shirts, and the floats express support for Israel. It is largely a nonpolitical and festive affair. In the 1980s, before my own march in the parade with my school, Papa and Nana took my brother and me to watch the parade. The grandstand was a packed area in the center of the parade route where a few bleachers had been set up for VIPs. Although as a kid I thought Papa was an important person, I hadn't realized how much of a VIP he was as far as the parade was concerned until we got to sit in the grandstand. Papa had a special connection with one of the parade organizers.

The Bar Mitzvah Guest

At my bar mitzvah party, a man about my grandparents' age came over to me in between dances. He asked: "Do you know who I am?"

I'm thinking, *um, no, but I don't want to insult any of my grandparents' friends*. He was obviously one of them; I just needed to guess which side of the family he was from. I knew they were mostly other survivors, adorable old men and women who loved seeing young Jewish kids running around.

Seeing my expression, the friendly man asked me a different question: "Do you know why I am here?" His voice inflected upward on "why."

That one was easy. "To help me celebrate my bar mitzvah?" I asked. Good call, genius, but no, that was not the answer he was looking for. Just as I sensed that the questioning was about to get more complicated, Papa rushed over with open arms, gave him a big hug, and exchanged some quick Yiddish.

"I see you met my grandson!" Papa said proudly, switching back to English.

"Yes!" the bar mitzvah guest said. And then directing the conversation back at me, he added, "I am here because of your grandfather." Obviously. However, as he said it, he gesticulated intensely, pointing at himself at "I," at the ground at "here," and at me at "your." He seemed unusually happy to be at my bar mitzvah. I politely thanked him for coming and stood quietly as they conversed joyfully in Yiddish.

I later learned more. While in the work camp at Gross-Rosen, Papa had a relatively plum job helping the Jewish doctor in the infirmary for part of the day (he worked in a steel mill for the larger part). One night, Papa found a young man sobbing and mumbling to no one in particular. Though misery was prevalent in the camp, no one really cried as most were numbed beyond that. Papa approached the man and asked why he was crying. The man told Papa that his brother had turned into a *Muselmann* [slang for "living bones"]. His only brother, wracked with hunger and pain, no longer had the will to eat or drink. The end was inevitable.

Papa consoled the man and told him not to worry. Telling others not to worry was a frequent consolation that people gave one another in the camp. However, "don't worry" rang hollow at this point. Not even Lamentations summed up the severity of this direst of times – "Maybe there is hope" (Book of Lamentations 3:29). "Hope" has inherent positive connotations, albeit remote and unrealistic. "Maybe there's hope?" – That's just too depressing to even think of considering a positive spin. But that's exactly where this man's mindset was at.

Later that evening, Papa quietly woke up the man with a cup of soup in hand. He had stolen it from the kitchen. The two of them sneaked out of the barracks and went to the infirmary, stealthily avoiding detection. When they got to the infirmary, the door was locked. Again, Papa said, "Don't worry," and he took the man to the back of the building, bent down underneath a window, and gestured to him to hop onto his back to climb through it. The man did exactly that and went through the infirmary to open the door for him up front. They found the man's brother. Sure enough, the brother was skin and bones – alive but barely alert and clearly awaiting death. Papa had to hold the brother's nose as he and the older brother poured the stolen soup down the younger brother's throat. The clandestine force-feeding went on for several nights until the brother got his wits about him again and was transferred back to the barracks. Even then, the brother still needed help and extra food, which Papa was able to smuggle in from his day job.

The Muselmann and his brother both survived and were delighted to attend my bar mitzvah.

One of the organizers of the parade was the same former Muselmann who later attended my bar mitzvah. When the grandkids heard the term "camps," they envisioned an outdoorsy experience where friends spent time in a bunkhouse and did activities together – not quite the experience Papa shared with his fellow prisoners. They all had an unbreakable bond from their "camp" days nonetheless.

As a token of appreciation, the man scored a few plum tickets to the parade for Papa and the family. Papa wore a straw fedora and a summer suit and tie. Always the tie. The tie was disarming because he looked so sharp and formal but was always so approachable. We enjoyed the music, the floats, and the overall pageantry and spectacle of the day every year.

One year, we encountered Neturei Karta protesting in a cordoned-off area on a side street along the parade route. Neturei Karta dress like other ultra-Orthodox Jews but hold the extreme belief that until God himself miraculously gathers Jews from the four corners of the world through the Messiah, Jews should not take any steps to set up a Jewish government in the Holy Land. A majority of nations voting in 1948 to establish the modern State of Israel was not miraculous enough for the Neturei Karta. Other ultra-Orthodox Jews also take issue to varying degrees with Israel's secular government, but they largely chalk up their differences as ideological and work within the system. The Neturei Karta actively side with antisemites who don't want Israel to exist as a political entity. We had to pass them to walk to the lot where Papa had parked his car.

Nothing aggravated Papa more than ungrateful, self-hating Jews – no matter whether they wore a black hat or no hat. These Neturei Karta wore black hats with Yasir Arafat-style kaffiyehs and were screaming something derogatory about Israel while holding placards about how "authentic" Jews don't back Israel.

"You would not be able to show your faces here today if it were not for Israel!" Papa scolded them. "You think you could enjoy your freedom of religion the way you do, even here in the US, if Israel did not exist? Such ingrates!" His point was that the freedoms of speech and religion that these people were enjoying in the United States would not entirely be possible but for Israel's existence. Knowing there is a Jewish state fortifies Jewish backbones around the world. Even if you disagree with the Israeli government, as a Jew, one has to be grateful for Israel's existence. The Jewish state was a pillar of strength sorely lacking earlier in Papa's life. Regardless of one's politics, acknowledging and appreciating Israel and its role in modern Jewish history had to be taken as a given. These "jokes," as Papa referred to them disdainfully, with the "J" rolling off his tongue to emphasize contempt, had it all wrong.

One or two of them engaged with him in a heated back-and-forth in Yiddish and Papa became increasingly agitated and disgusted as the conversation continued. Nana encouraged him and the kids to move along, which they did. Not quite out of earshot, one of the Neturei Karta-niks tried a different tack and mockingly asked Papa if he even prayed.

"I put my tefillin on much earlier than you did today," Papa snapped and moved on. The hypocrisy of seeming to outwardly care about observance while also outwardly denying the basic precept of gratitude could not have been more palpable. And he let them know it.

The Shabbos Elevator

Unfortunately, the Neturei Karta do not have a monopoly on being hypocritical Jews. In the high-rise building where Nana and Papa lived in Fort Lee, New Jersey, a service elevator was programmed to enable religious residents who observe the Jewish Sabbath to refrain from performing prohibited activity (pushing the elevator buttons ignites a spark of electricity, which is considered work) while also giving all residents the convenience of riding it. It was preprogrammed to go from the lobby to the top floor, and then to stop on every other floor. First, the odd floors, and then the even floors on the next trip. There were preset times for the automated service, starting Friday evening until 10 p.m. and again Saturday morning through afternoon.

The other three elevators operated normally. The wait for the other elevators was marginally impacted, if at all. Those who wanted the

Shabbos elevator knew to go to the service elevator entrance. Those who wished to ride the elevator as normal did so. The arrangement worked well for several years. Some religious Jews actually moved to the building because of the convenience of being able to take the Shabbos elevator instead of the steps. It was a selling point for some apartments, especially on the upper floors.

However, in 2011, some members of the co-op board brought the issue of the Shabbos elevator up at a meeting. Some Jewish residents did not appreciate the accommodation the building was making for their more observant brethren. One woman made a motion to do away with presetting times for the service elevator to run on auto on Saturdays. "It's a hassle for the workers in the building to do this every week," she said. "And dedicating an entire elevator for this increases my wait time for an elevator; we should not have to do this for a few people." The condescension and disdain of this woman for her observant neighbors were striking. Her tone and demeanor were transparent.

None of her arguments were accurate or compelling. First, it was more than "a few people" who would be shut in every Saturday if not for the Shabbos elevator. The adjustment to the elevator was minimal and not much of a hassle. Most people did not notice or care about the service elevator being used this way, and it cost the building nothing extra to accommodate.

The woman's few supporters nodded in agreement. "Comments, anyone?" asked the condominium board president. Papa was relatively frail at this point. A few months post-heart surgery, he got around using a cane – his "stick," as he called it – and walked slower than his preferred speedy pace. Nonetheless, he made his way up to the podium and grabbed the mic.

"I am a United States citizen for over 55 years," he said. "I have been living in this building for over 30 years. I appreciate and respect everyone. This is a beautiful place to live and I get along with everyone nicely. I would never have thought that I would see, in my own building where I live, such a dislike for religious practice. This elevator is so important."

"But Jack, I'm Jewish and we don't need this," she responded, attempting to explain that her motion to stop the Shabbos elevator was an administrative move for the common good.

Jack snapped back, "Then you are a Jewish antisemite! And you should be ashamed of yourself."

The normally staid room erupted in raucous applause. A few even cried at seeing the survivor speak from the heart. The motion failed.

Papa sat down and shrugged with a bit of a humble swagger. "She does not want so many Orthodox people here," he said. "That's her problem. This is the United States. Anyone who wants can live where they want. I told her like it is. She has no right to keep people from practicing religion. What a joke this woman is!"

Testimony
Only In America

A letter from the Consul of the Federal Republic of Germany dated April 29, 1991, made its way to Papa at his home address. It read:

Dear Mr. Wimmer:

Please be advised that you have been named as a witness in a Nazi war crimes case being tried in the regional court in Stuttgart, Germany.

The defendant in this case is the German national Josef Schwammberger.

At the request of the court, you are hereby invited to give your testimony on: Tuesday, June 18, 1991 at 10 a.m. (18th floor)

At this Consulate General, Members of the Regional Court in Stuttgart will be present at your hearing.

Very truly yours,

Axel John

Consul

Schwammberger, the SS lieutenant who had served as commander of Nazi labor camps in Poland between 1942 and 1944, was charged in the deaths of more than 3,000 people. After World War II, Schwammberger fled to Argentina, became an Argentinian citizen, and lived there under his own name. In 1987, he was arrested for his wartime activities and extradited to Germany in 1990 to stand trial. After his arrest, the Simon Wiesenthal Center, a human rights organization that famously hunted down Nazis, helped to track down survivors who may have witnessed some of Schwammberger's atrocities. Papa's name came up several times as someone who personally witnessed Schwammberger in action.

By 1990, Papa had traveled to many countries to attend and lecture at dental conventions. Though invited several times to attend dental conventions in Germany, he never went. Even though present-day Germany was different from World War II Germany, he'd had enough. Papa saw no need to support that nation in any way. He never drove a German car. Going to Germany was certainly out of the question.

With firm conviction, Papa responded to Germany's invitation with a caveat: "I will testify, but I will not go to Germany. I am an American citizen now. You come to me, in New York where it's a free country." Papa's bold ask was not surprising. What was surprising is that they agreed to it. The entire trial team (except for the defendant himself), including the judge, prosecuting attorneys, defending attorneys, and court officers, recreated the Stuttgart courtroom inside the German consulate in Manhattan solely to accommodate this adamant witness.

My brother, Daniel, Papa's oldest grandchild, who was then 22 years old, accompanied Papa to the proceeding. Daniel wrote about the trial experience immediately afterward:

July 1992
by Daniel Schloss

My Grandfather is a vibrant person who energizes a room when he enters it. Even when he speaks about the horrors he endured in World War II Poland about the entire family that he lost, about his unthinkable physical and psychological anguish, he nearly always retains his composure and self-assurance. He channels his searing grief into an urgent reminder of what needs to be done now in order to ensure that the awful images etched in his memory do not die with him; however, I had always suspected that he held some things back, that some stories were simply too painful to recount under normal conditions. Although he answered any questions about the war put to him by his children and grandchildren, after a point we did not know what to ask.

When the headlines appeared several years back announcing the arrest of Josef Schwammberger, a former SS officer who had escaped to Argentina, I had no idea that my Grandfather had any connection to him. It was not until April of 1991 that Papa told me that he had seen Schwammberger murder the rabbi of the town of Wieliczka in front of 1,200 people at the close of Yom Kippur in 1942. He asked me to accompany him to the German Consulate in New York where he was going to testify in a special session of Schwammberger's trial which was being conducted under strict guard. Several judges and Schwammberger's defense attorney were being flown in to question him. As usual, Papa steeled himself and resolved to tell his heartbreaking story clearly and without hesitation.

About a month later, we took a cab from his office to the consulate, where the people were polite to the point of being obsequious. Once the proceedings were called to order the Consul (who acted as an interpreter, even though my Grandfather understands and speaks German very well) explained that this was to be a closed session and that my presence would therefore not be allowed unless my Grandfather could offer a compelling reason for it.

"I want my grandson to hear what I am going to say," Papa boldly asserted.

The Consul retorted that "intellectual curiosity is not good enough, Sir."

There was a brief pause as the attorney from the Simon Wiesenthal Center whispered in my Grandfather's ear.

"I would like my grandson to be here for psychological support."

This was deemed an acceptable reason.

As Papa spoke, the Consul interrupted periodically to give brief official summaries of the points made in the testimony to the court reporter. These summaries constitute the entire content of the transcript of record, so that the vigor and emotion that would have come through to any reader of a verbatim account was lost. Instead, the transcript became more like a legal document which, although factually accurate, was stiff, overly formal, and not truly representative of what Papa actually said.

First, he spoke of the arrival of the Nazis in Wieliczka, his hometown. Thirty-two people were immediately rounded up and later shot to death in the woods outside of the town. Later on, the Nazis performed one of their infamous "selections," in which Papa was separated from his parents, brothers, and sister. He ran to join them but was beaten back and never saw them again. Papa barely flinched as he recounted these awful events. He only began to expose his emotional open wounds when they asked him about his encounter with Schwammberger.

The SS officer came to the area where Papa's group was working at the Stalowa Wola labor camp in Rozwadow at about noon on Yom Kippur and demanded a list of all those in the group. Papa spoke German and was therefore ordered by Schwammberger to write down the names. Later in the day, he realized that since the Rabbi was in the group and since Schwammberger had only asked for a list from this particular group, an informer must have told him about the Rabbi's presence. Papa resolved not to turn over the names, and one of the only verbatim sections of the transcript recorded the words he spoke to a fellow prisoner before the fateful evening roll call: "I have lost my family. I don't have anything to worry about, and I will not do it." Unfortunately, Papa's courage could not help the Rabbi.

At the roll call, Schwammberger ordered "Frenkel" to step forward. There were two men other than the Rabbi who had that surname, and each of them stepped forward before Schwammberger sent them back into the line and screamed, "Rabbi Frenkel is to step forward." Once he did, Schwammberger declared the Rabbi guilty of sabotage, shot him dead, and then ordered the body to be taken away in a wheelbarrow.

By this point in the testimony, the Consul had tried to interrupt several times, but Papa insisted on continuing as the tears welled up. When he finally paused for a moment, the Council and the judges were eager to know other details – what kind of a handgun had Schwammberger used, a Mauser or a .22? (Papa replied that he knew only that it was a handgun.) They pressed on – where exactly had the bullet hit? Was the roll call area on level ground? They asked similar asinine questions, although during the short break that Papa requested, they were again excruciatingly polite. One particularly galling line in the transcript which is actually a response pieced together from several of Papa's almost angry retorts was "Until the end of my stay in Rozwadow, I did not see any more cases when Schwammberger committed crimes personally." I wondered whether the ludicrous questions which led to this irrelevant pseudo-statement were meant to demonstrate that the defendant had since had a change of heart. In response to further outrageous questions, Papa explained that the charge of sabotage was unfounded, that the Rabbi was indistinguishable in appearance from the other prisoners, and that Schwammberger and the other Nazis did not care whether anyone fasted on Yom Kippur, as long as they worked – which the Rabbi did.

Though he spoke German, Papa testified in English via a translator. At one point, Papa perceived that the German translator was mistranslating his words. In German, he castigated the interpreter. "We are not in Gestapo Germany; we are in the United States of America; you better translate what I say and not what you want me to say."

After identifying Schwammberger in some photographs, Papa signed his name to the transcript, collected himself, and acknowledged the judges, who were clearly impressed with him and were politely sympathetic. Once the session was closed, they spoke with him in German and noted that they were particularly struck by the fact that Schwammberger had clearly sought out his victim because of his status as a religious communal leader.

Papa turned to me when we left and put his hand on my shoulder. "You remember this," he said, "you write this down."

Quiet Joy

When my eldest, my daughter, was born in 1998, we were overjoyed. For my grandparents, this first great-grandchild on both sides represented the validation of hope and brought tremendous joy. In typical fashion, Nana and Papa Wimmer were the first visitors to the hospital. En route to a dental convention in Las Vegas, they got the news and took a detour to the hospital before heading to John F. Kennedy International Airport. In this short visit, they gushed with palpable joy.

Genuine Kvelling

A few hours later, the next round of kvellers arrived. Grandma and Grandpa Schloss came with my aunt Fran and uncle Bruce. The baby girl was sleeping in the nursery and was available for viewing through the window like a puppy in a pet store. Four sets of joyful eyes peering through the glass stood and stared for a couple of minutes. Grandpa broke the silence with: "I think she's gonna be a lawyer." Not exactly sure what prompted that, though I'll make an educated guess. Grandpa Shaya came to this country on a boat with the clothes on his back, a young wife, a little boy, and little else. Grandpa and Grandma worked hard to raise that boy and his little brother, who both went to public school, high school, college, and eventually law school. That boy on the boat grew up, got married, and had two boys of his own. Those two boys went to yeshiva day school, high school, college, law school, and eventually became lawyers. Grandpa perceived becoming a lawyer as the pinnacle of the American dream. As a "greener" who came to American shores not knowing English, he was enormously proud of his two sons and two grandsons, who all make their livelihoods via mastery of English.

Coming back to this baby girl on the other side of the glass, just by being there, she caused emotion and reflection across multiple generations. Grandpa was reflecting on his journey, and the lawyer remark was an expression of hope and confidence in the brightness of the future.

When we named the baby Miriam, Grandpa took to calling her Miriam ll, or Little Miriam, for his dear mother. During the war, Grandpa had relied heavily on his mother's urgent blessings from when they hastily parted ways after Yom Kippur 1941 to steel himself with purpose. Giving up would have been an easy choice, but now, decades later, young Shaya had become a great-grandfather of a girl named for his mother. Tissues anyone?

Shalom Aleichem, Reb Yid!

In 2012, Papa had a mild heart attack that led to bypass surgery. Thankfully, the doctors at NYU Langone Hospital gave him expert attention and care. Due to the surgery, it was difficult for Papa to communicate as he was hooked up to various medical apparatuses. On one rotation, a physician with a *kippah* [head covering] came to check in on Papa. While all the doctors and nurses at the hospital gave exceptional care, Papa felt an additional level of comfort and pride that a Jewish doctor was also involved.

That feeling quickly dissipated. Papa saw the doctor look at him and then his chart, then at him again, and again at the chart. With a birth year in 1923, blue eyes, light hair, and a German-sounding last name, Papa realized what must have been going on in this doctor's mind. With pursed lips and a bit of a scowl, the doctor dutifully and efficiently began to change the dressings and tubing. There was no smile or empathetic small talk; only efficient care.

This doctor thinks I must be a Nazi, Papa thought in horror.

As soon as the doctor removed the tubing, Papa mustered a *"Shalom aleichem reb yid!"* [loosely translated as "Greetings, my dear fellow Jew!"] Immediately, the doctor's disposition changed. Papa had correctly intuited that the doctor had made several quick, incorrect assumptions about his past. A broad smile, a chuckle, and some comforting small talk ensued.

Seder

On Passover, the overarching theme is to imagine ourselves as having left the bondage of Egypt ourselves. With any of my grandparents, that aspect of our *Seder* [the festive meal celebrating the holiday] did not take much imagining. With obvious parallels between cruel task masters of yesteryear and those he had personally experienced, Papa usually stuck to the script of the *Haggadah* (the traditional book used jointly as a conversation starter and prayer book at the Seder). There were times at a Passover meal (usually lunch, not the Seder) when Papa would tell us some of his experiences during the Holocaust.

In the afternoons, Papa was like one of the kids. Papa, my brother, and I made up a song as we threw couch pillows across the room to each other – "Over to Dana, over to Jona... to Papa!" – switching up directions and how hard we threw while trying to avoid other family members who might not have sanctioned the activity.

At the Seder itself, Papa usually seemed like he was in a rush. He enjoyed the grandkids' school-prompted riffs on the Exodus story but also playfully encouraged us to move it along.

Except at the end of the Seder. Late at night, after we had read the whole Haggadah, eaten a festive meal with all the ritualistic foods, including matzah and four cups of wine, and after the last songs found in most Haggadahs were sung, most people end their seders. Not us. On the back page of the red and yellow Haggadahs we used, there were some additional "optional" songs. Our seder did not finish until we sang *Hatikvah* (literally, "The Hope") – Israel's national anthem.

One part of our Seder was not like others. While most of the seder was conducted sitting and reclining as free people do, when Papa led us in Hatikvah at the conclusion of the Seder, we all stood at soldier-like attention as we sang. Hatkivah reflects the Jewish people's 2,000-year-old hope of returning to the land of Israel, restoring it, and reclaiming it as a free and sovereign nation. Flawed as it may be at times, Israel gives Jews around the world a renewed backbone that Jews over the millennia had only prayed for.

Papa first heard Hatikvah as the official anthem of the Zionist Beitar movement in his youth and then heard it as Israel's national anthem. Papa had personally witnessed the arc of Jewish history pivot and proudly mandated that the Seder conclude with Hatikvah. No matter how late it was or how tired we were, no one left the table until after Hatikvah. What better way to express the message that the meal we had just finished was not merely a relic of past practice? The Seder was an expression of remembering our people's collective journey. While generations past only dreamed of being able to say "Next year in Jerusalem" and having the prospect be realistic, for us, sitting at the Seder in the late 20th and early 21st centuries, that hope was indeed a viable option.

You could see the emotion on Papa's face as he stood at attention with fists firmly planted on the table while looking around the table as young and old joined in Hatikvah. His overall demeanor as we sang projected that here stood a man, defiant, resolute, proud, and thankful – all at once.

After the relatively intense Hatikvah, Papa would start washing dishes with a playful challenge to all, "I vash, who's vishing with me?" And the race was on to keep pace. The considerable vigor with which he happily washed the dishes – usually starting after 1 a.m. – set the tone. The rest of us dried and reset the table for the next meal. He washed so quickly that we hardly knew where the time flew. It was always good family bonding time. One year, I think it was 2002 or 2003, my daughter was four or five and surprisingly still awake at the end of the Seder when Papa issued his dishes challenge. She raced to move a step stool across the kitchen floor toward the sink, grabbed a towel, and turned on the sink – all before he got to the sink himself. Finally, he had a partner who could move at his pace.

By *Pesach* [Passover] in April 2017, Papa's health was in steady decline. Uncharacteristically and painfully, he had to excuse himself from the table not long after the Seder began. Of course, we continued the Seder with Papa resting in a nearby bedroom, but it already wasn't the same. We sang Hatikvah without Papa presiding, and there was no post-Seder giddy dishwashing session. Soon after the holiday, we were advised by medical professionals to focus on ensuring he was comfortable. That is what we did. Still strong-willed, Papa did not want to go to hospice or a facility of any kind and insisted on a diet of vanilla ice cream. While some days were better than others, he always maintained the glint in his eyes. But the pep in his step was gone and he spent most of the day in bed. Vanilla ice cream flowed freely. The last time I spoke to Papa was on Mother's Day, 2017. The immediate family gathered in Nana and Papa's apartment. He was alert but in bed. I went to his side with my wife.

"Hey Jona, you kiss your wife, it's Mother's Day," he mustered in a loudish whisper as he winked at me. The twinkle was still there. The strength? Not so much. We laughed and stayed with him until he got a bit more tired.

Over the next few days, Papa's body steadily proceeded to shut down. Doctors assured the family that he was as comfortable as could be, but nothing more could be done medically. His dear wife, son, daughter, son-in-law, and two older grandsons took turns at his bedside. On the night of the 28th of Iyar on the Hebrew calendar, the 50th anniversary of the reunification of Jerusalem, the family got together at Papa's bedside, stood resolutely, and sang Hatikvah with Papa present one last time.

Shiva

During shiva for Papa, many people came to visit my mother, grandmother, and uncle to pay their last respects. As a grandchild of the deceased, I was technically (according to Jewish law) not a "mourner," but the many people who came and visited brought me and my entire family comfort. A few exchanges I had with some visitors stand out.

On the way up to the apartment, I greeted the longtime doorman. He knew Papa well. Before I got to the elevator, he stopped me. "Your Grandpa was a great man," he said. "You don't even know." I appreciated the sentiment, but really? I don't even know? What does the doorman know that I do not?

"Thank you," I said, "I know he enjoyed talking to you and he appreciated all your help."

"That's my job, and it was my honor to know him."

He continued: "Some people in this building, they don't even look at me and my co-workers in the eye; we're like lowly servants to some of them. Your Grandpa, he treated me and everyone else here more like family, with respect, and we all loved him. I want you to know that. It's him and the few people like him that make working in this business worth it. He was really that special. I miss him already."

Wow, I thought.

Upstairs, the ebb and flow of visitors was constant. My brother, sister-in-law, and my wife and I all took turns making sure that our grandmother was comfortable and not overwhelmed by the crowd. At one point during the day, when there were relatively few visitors, the door opened quietly, followed by a loud wail. I thought someone had been hurt. Well, on a certain level, the person was, just not physically. A 60-plus-year-old man came to pay respects and could not control his raw emotion as he entered the shiva home. My mother and I looked at each other – who is this guy? I offered him some water and was politely rebuffed. After he calmed himself, he sat before my grandmother and mother.

"He was like a father to me and I miss him so!" he said. That seemed to be a running theme.

The man was a successful businessperson who was not religiously observant. He lived in the building by himself and had made his way to the shul across the street for the High Holidays one year. Papa engaged with him, found out his life story, and invited him for Shabbat meals. He often joined Nana and Papa on Shabbat evenings or afternoons after services.

"Your husband said something to me that changed my life," he told my grandmother.

"Businessman to businessman, he asked me: 'What's the point of all this if you can't give, if you can't make an impact with what God has given you?' He taught me so much about living and about giving.

"One night, I get a call from Jack. He said that he and Jack Zwas (another survivor and member of the same shul) would be picking me up in a few minutes and that I shouldn't ask so many questions. They picked me up and we went to someone's apartment. Five or six of us around a table. And Jack says, "The shul is at a critical stage. We need to raise money to buy the property next door and to fund expansion. No one leaves this table until we are all committed to contribute according to our means.

"'The shul needs us; *am yisrael* [the people of Israel] needs us. Let's do it,' was the overall serious tone. Everyone at that table ponied up at least six figures that night and spearheaded an aggressive fundraising campaign that resulted in the beautiful shul we have today. I never would have done that but for Jack."

Thanks to Papa, the man extended his philanthropic interests well beyond the shul. He proudly knows his legacy will live on. He apologized unnecessarily for the exuberant entrance. He just couldn't control himself as the deep loss of a life mentor seared his heart.

Whether a doorman or a CEO with a name on the door, Papa's outgoing, honest, and loving nature made people of all walks of life feel comfortable with him.

The third-most memorable shiva visitor (to me) was the son of a man who had survived the Gross-Rosen work camp with Papa. This man's father, Jacob "Kuba" Deutscher, was a few years older than Papa and was also originally from the Kraków area. As the son was waiting his turn to speak with my grandmother, I introduced myself. We had met a few times before but I was unsure if he remembered who I was.

"I don't know you well, and I'm sure you are a fantastic person, like the rest of your family," the son said to me. "Just know, though, that nothing you will do will ever, ever compare to your grandfather. He was on a level so far above us all."

While some might have found this to be a strange greeting, I knew exactly what he was referring to. At least in part.

In the camp, Papa was caught smuggling food to some of the prisoners in the infirmary. As punishment, one of the Nazis picked Kuba to mete out punishment. Kuba was told to slap Papa as hard as he could. Under threat of additional punishment or even death, Kuba had no choice.

"Again! Harder!" Papa remembered hearing the orders being barked several times as Kuba reluctantly had to comply.

After the beating, Papa was not broken. Quite the contrary. He was more resolved to help others get through those trying times, starting with his friend Kuba, who felt terrible about having to slap his friend so hard. Papa told Kuba that he did not hold him responsible for what had just happened.

Yes, Kuba's son was right.

Senior Living

In his last years, Sam Schloss's mind remained sharp and could still drive a car; two precious lifelines at his independent care facility. Until he could no longer drive himself, he did not complain much about the food as he cooked for himself. He sat with others during meals, attended prayer services and off-site and on-site card games. To stay game-ready, he played cards with his fabulous aide Kathy, tallying each win and loss on a note pad with some light trash-talking to spice it up. He went to events at the facility and watched TV to keep up with current events and the Mets. His children Jack and Betty lived nearby. His children Bruce and Fran dutifully came every Sunday; during baseball season they commiserated or celebrated Mets losses and wins together. The grandchildren called and visited regularly. Shaya missed Grandma terribly but he was not bored. The aides and staff knew him well and appreciated his readily shared acute observations about the goings-on at the facility.

Every now and then Shaya forgot the key to his room and would lock himself out. I once met Grandpa Shaya in the dining room and walked him back to his apartment. "I think I left the key inside again, Tatele."

"Should I call the front desk Grandpa?"

"Feh! Don't bother."

There was no worry or need to call the front desk though so long as he had his wallet on him.

Ever resourceful and self-sufficient, Grandpa picked the lock on his own door with a credit card.

The Covid Funeral

In late March 2020, as hospitals became inundated with Covid-19 patients, Governor Cuomo issued a directive to nursing homes and adult-care facilities. No hospital patients with Covid-19 diagnoses could be denied admission at a facility based on a Covid-19 diagnosis. The American Health Care Association released a statement on March 28, 2020 saying that the Governor's "approach will introduce the highly contagious virus into more nursing homes... and ultimately, a higher number of deaths... Issuing such an order is a mistake...

Like all adult care facilities, Grandpa Shaya's adult care facility grappled with how to best keep the elderly safe from the new, horrible virus. By April 2020, no one but aides and health care workers could visit but, paradoxically, the facility was also compelled to take back in Covid-19 residents from hospitals. I called Grandpa in early April 2020 to check in. "Well, I'm feeling okay but I'm sorry to tell you that your friend's mother – she just died from the Covid." I had heard already. He continued, "I just saw her last week; we were sitting by the doctor's office downstairs here." I did not know that part.

Grandpa's aide Kathy dutifully came every morning even as the world was adapting to Covid. About a week after my phone call, she found Grandpa on his apartment floor as she entered. We did not know that balance issues, dizziness and fatigue were often observed in older Covid-19 patients. Grandpa lasted a few days in the hospital before succumbing to Covid on his half-birthday at the age of 97.

Government mandates allowed no more than ten participants at a funeral. As my father and uncle needed to recite Kaddish, we needed exactly a minyan of ten. With Shaya's two sons, two grandsons, two of his great-grandsons and a rabbi, we needed three more to complete the minyan. I posted that on Facebook and was immediately inundated with off-line requests to volunteer. Shaya never got to sit shiva for his parents or siblings and once thought it possible that he might be the last Jew on the planet – and now dozens were clamoring to join three generations of Shaya's descendants to complete the minyan at his funeral. In a surreal funeral in which all precautions were taken, Shaya Schloss was laid to rest next to his dear Feigele.

As was the fashion of the times, we followed up 30 days later with a dignified memorial Zoom session where hundreds of people paid respects to Shaya Schloss.

The COVID-19 Minyan

There is an interesting discussion in the Talmud among several rabbis opining about what single verse in the Torah best distills Judaism's ideals into one concise, important directive. Of all the lofty verses – "*Shema Yisrael* [Hear O Israel]," "You shall love thy neighbor as thyself," "Respect your father and mother" – none of them were deemed by the rabbis of the Talmud as most important. To them, the most important was: "The one lamb you shall bring in the morning and the second lamb you shall bring in the afternoon."

How does a seemingly humdrum verse about bringing daily sacrifices get the title of "most important"? Judaism values consistency over time as a hallmark of the faith. One who truly seeks to keep the tenets of the Jewish faith does so by serving God in all aspects of daily life. This is not an easy task; hence, the lofty Talmudic accolade.

When COVID hit, the world came to a screeching halt in so many ways. Like all other public spaces, shul stopped altogether for several months. Overnight, people who had attended synagogue daily for decades could not. Prayers over Zoom are not the same as being in the same room as others, both from a *halachic* [Jewish legal] and practical perspective.

As people acclimated to the distancing of pandemic life, daily synagogue-goers created ad hoc, socially distanced minyanim in backyards and driveways all over Jewish neighborhoods. Backyard tents proliferated around town. With people working from home (or otherwise unemployed and home), getting the requisite ten for the quorum was not the biggest challenge. That designation went to coping with the weather. Not rain, not sleet, nor dead of winter kept the diehard minyan-goers from their appointed daily rounds of communal prayer in Jewish neighborhoods across the country. As people started to go back to shul, the outdoor minyanim closed one by one, each holding out until the mainstays felt comfortable going back indoors. The grandchildren and great-grandchildren of Romek/Jack and Sala/Sally, and those of Shaya/Sam and Feigele, all participated in outdoor minyanim. Eventually, as the pandemic restrictions eased, the backyard minyanim folded their tents and headed back to shul. One minyan with an immunocompromised regular shul-goer was reluctant to go back inside too quickly and the community obliged until this person was ready to go back indoors. One great-grandson was singled out in his shul's weekly bulletin:

The successful completion of the minyan in the Rosens' backyard gives us the opportunity to thank the many families who loyally davened there through rain, cold and heat. I especially wish to recognize Chananel Chudnoff, Mordechai and Akiva Gelernter, Yoel Gellman and Yehoshua Schloss, our young *chevra* [brotherhood] who loyally attended and responsibly tended to the minyan, through all seasons, trading in comfort and hanging with friends for the mitzvah of leading the *tzibbur* [congregation] and providing for others. May we continue to see much *nachas* [spiritual pleasure] from you and continue to take great pride in your accomplishments. Welcome back!

This snippet was emailed to membership on the fourth of Iyar 2781 – exactly on Grandpa Shaya's yahrzeit – the anniversary on the Hebrew calendar of his passing. I read it and paused as the historical importance of this mundane announcement hit me. Grandpa survived World War II on his own in the forest and barns through rain, cold, snow, and heat, all while thinking he might be the last living Jew. And here, his great-grandson, who had helped this outdoor prayer group thrive while exposed to the elements, was being given a pat on the back.

"Through all seasons, trading in comfort and hanging with friends for the mitzvah of leading the tzibbur and providing for others" – every part of that sentence was so far beyond the pale of Grandpa's imagination decades earlier. From Yom Kippur 1942 to early 1945, through all seasons, Grandpa had no comfort and no friends. Quite the opposite. Armed only with his wits and ability to work hard, he miraculously made it through. The barns he slept in on frigid nights were infested with vermin that gave him horrible rashes.

The few "friends" from his public school days tried to turn him in. He had to bite his tongue – hard – and hide when he learned of his sister's murder to keep from tipping anyone off. He had only his mother's parting words, pleading with him to do all he could to survive, to give him the confidence and strength to outwit the enemy.

Comparatively, COVID-19 lockdowns were a piece of cake. To be forced to stay at home with heat, indoor plumbing, a warm bed with clean sheets, a refrigerator with food, and Wi-Fi for the better part of a year seems quaint in comparison. Nonetheless, each generation is faced with its own challenges, and in 2020, Shaya and Feigele's and Romek and Sala's descendants and neighbors were challenged with running a socially distanced outdoor minyan to make sure that an immunocompromised neighbor would not miss out on communal prayer.

"*Hineh ma tov u'mah na'im, shevet achim gam yachad* [Behold how good and how pleasant it is for brothers to dwell together]." (Psalms 133:11)

Sally Wimmer at a Park Dental exhibit booth at a dental convention (1981)

Jack Wimmer picking out a citron (an "etrog") in preparation for the holiday of Sukkot, Lower East Side of Manhattan (2014)

Shaya serving up matzah ball for soup (2016)

Grandma Fay Schloss with great-grandson Eli
(2002)

Jack Wimmer and Senator Joseph Lieberman

The extended Wimmer family

The extended Schloss family

Great-grandparents in sweaters; great-grandkids in pool (Florida, 2006)

Two grandfathers (2013)

Sally Wimmer enjoying two great-grandsons (2010)

Shaya Schloss getting ready to watch the Mets (2016)

Shaya Schloss (Top row left to right) with his granddaughter Emily and great-grandchildren, Miriam, Leora, Jonah, Ori (Bottom row) - Shua and Eli

ABOUT THE AUTHOR

Jonathan Schloss is the proud grandson of Sam and Fay Schloss and Jack and Sally Wimmer. He is profoundly grateful as a "3rd Gen" member that most of his children knew and remember all of his grandparents. Jonathan is the managing attorney of Schloss and Schloss PC, a law firm he runs with father, Jack Schloss. He lives in New Jersey with his wife Devorah (Lahasky) and is the proud father of Miriam, Eli & Devorah (Burg), Yehoshua and Ori, and the proud grandfather of Ahuva Faiga.

AMSTERDAM PUBLISHERS
HOLOCAUST LIBRARY

The series **Holocaust Survivor Memoirs World War II** consists of the following autobiographies of survivors:

Outcry. Holocaust Memoirs, by Manny Steinberg

Hank Brodt Holocaust Memoirs. A Candle and a Promise, by Deborah Donnelly

The Dead Years. Holocaust Memoirs, by Joseph Schupack

Rescued from the Ashes. The Diary of Leokadia Schmidt, Survivor of the Warsaw Ghetto, by Leokadia Schmidt

My Lvov. Holocaust Memoir of a twelve-year-old Girl, by Janina Hescheles

Remembering Ravensbrück. From Holocaust to Healing, by Natalie Hess

Wolf. A Story of Hate, by Zeev Scheinwald with Ella Scheinwald

Save my Children. An Astonishing Tale of Survival and its Unlikely Hero, by Leon Kleiner with Edwin Stepp

Holocaust Memoirs of a Bergen-Belsen Survivor & Classmate of Anne Frank, by Nanette Blitz Konig

Defiant German - Defiant Jew. A Holocaust Memoir from inside the Third Reich, by Walter Leopold with Les Leopold

In a Land of Forest and Darkness. The Holocaust Story of two Jewish Partisans, by Sara Lustigman Omelinski

Holocaust Memories. Annihilation and Survival in Slovakia, by Paul Davidovits

From Auschwitz with Love. The Inspiring Memoir of Two Sisters' Survival, Devotion and Triumph Told by Manci Grunberger Beran & Ruth Grunberger Mermelstein, by Daniel Seymour

Remetz. Resistance Fighter and Survivor of the Warsaw Ghetto, by Jan Yohay Remetz

My March Through Hell. A Young Girl's Terrifying Journey to Survival, by Halina Kleiner with Edwin Stepp

Roman's Journey, by Roman Halter

Beyond Borders. Escaping the Holocaust and Fighting the Nazis. 1938-1948, by Rudi Haymann

The Engineers. A memoir of survival through World War II in Poland and Hungary, by Henry Reiss

Spark of Hope. An Autobiography, by Luba Wrobel Goldberg

Footnote to History. From Hungary to America. The Memoir of a Holocaust Survivor, by Andrew Laszlo

Farewell Atlantis. Recollections, by Valentīna Freimane

The Courtyard. A memoir, by Benjamin Parket and Alexa Morris

The Mulberry Tree. The story of a life before and after the Holocaust, by Iboja Wandall-Holm

The Boy in the Back. A True Story of Survival in Auschwitz and Mauthausen, as told to Fern Lebo by Jan Blumenstein

Beneath the Lightless Sky. Surviving the Holocaust in the Sewers of Lvov, by Ignacy Chiger

Mendel Run, by Milton H. Schwartz

The series **Holocaust Survivor True Stories**
consists of the following biographies:

Among the Reeds. The true story of how a family survived the Holocaust, by Tammy Bottner

A Holocaust Memoir of Love & Resilience. Mama's Survival from Lithuania to America, by Ettie Zilber

Living among the Dead. My Grandmother's Holocaust Survival Story of Love and Strength, by Adena Bernstein Astrowsky

Heart Songs. A Holocaust Memoir, by Barbara Gilford

Shoes of the Shoah. The Tomorrow of Yesterday, by Dorothy Pierce

Hidden in Berlin. A Holocaust Memoir, by Evelyn Joseph Grossman

Separated Together. The Incredible True WWII Story of Soulmates Stranded an Ocean Apart, by Kenneth P. Price, Ph.D.

The Man Across the River. The incredible story of one man's will to survive the Holocaust, by Zvi Wiesenfeld

If Anyone Calls, Tell Them I Died. A Memoir, by Emanuel (Manu) Rosen

The House on Thrömerstrasse. A Story of Rebirth and Renewal in the Wake of the Holocaust, by Ron Vincent

Dancing with my Father. His hidden past. Her quest for truth. How Nazi Vienna shaped a family's identity, by Jo Sorochinsky

The Story Keeper. Weaving the Threads of Time and Memory - A Memoir, by Fred Feldman

Krisia's Silence. The Girl who was not on Schindler's List, by Ronny Hein

Defying Death on the Danube. A Holocaust Survival Story, by Debbie J. Callahan with Henry Stern

A Doorway to Heroism. A decorated German-Jewish Soldier who became an American Hero, by W. Jack Romberg

The Shoemaker's Son. The Life of a Holocaust Resister, by Laura Beth Bakst

The Redhead of Auschwitz. A True Story, by Nechama Birnbaum

Land of Many Bridges. My Father's Story, by Bela Ruth Samuel Tenenholtz

Creating Beauty from the Abyss. The Amazing Story of Sam Herciger, Auschwitz Survivor and Artist, by Lesley Ann Richardson

On Sunny Days We Sang. A Holocaust Story of Survival and Resilience, by Jeannette Grunhaus de Gelman

Painful Joy. A Holocaust Family Memoir, by Max J. Friedman

I Give You My Heart. A True Story of Courage and Survival, by Wendy Holden

In the Time of Madmen, by Mark A. Prelas

Monsters and Miracles. Horror, Heroes and the Holocaust, by Ira Wesley Kitmacher

Flower of Vlora. Growing up Jewish in Communist Albania, by Anna Kohen

Aftermath: Coming of Age on Three Continents. A Memoir, by Annette Libeskind Berkovits

Not a real Enemy. The True Story of a Hungarian Jewish Man's Fight for Freedom, by Robert Wolf

Zaidy's War. Four Armies, Three Continents, Two Brothers. One Man's Impossible Story of Endurance, by Martin Bodek

The Glassmaker's Son. Looking for the World my Father left behind in Nazi Germany, by Peter Kupfer

The Apprentice of Buchenwald. The True Story of the Teenage Boy Who Sabotaged Hitler's War Machine, by Oren Schneider

Good for a Single Journey, by Helen Joyce

Burying the Ghosts. She escaped Nazi Germany only to have her life torn apart by the woman she saved from the camps: her mother, by Sonia Case

American Wolf. From Nazi Refugee to American Spy. A True Story, by Audrey Birnbaum

Bipolar Refugee. A Saga of Survival and Resilience, by Peter Wiesner

In the Wake of Madness. My Family's Escape from the Nazis, by Bettie Lennett Denny

Before the Beginning and After the End, by Hymie Anisman

I Will Give Them an Everlasting Name. Jacksonville's Stories of the Holocaust, by Samuel Cox

Hiding in Holland. A Resistance Memoir, by Shulamit Reinharz

The Ghosts on the Wall. A Grandson's Memoir of the Holocaust, by Kenneth D. Wald

Thirteen in Auschwitz. My grandmother's fight to stay human, by Lauren Meyerowitz Port

The Jewish Woman Who Fought the Nazis. Bep Schaap-Bedak's life during the Holocaust in Holland, by Eli Schaap

Voices of Resilience. An Anthology of Stories written by Children of Holocaust Survivors, Edited by Deborah (Devora) Ross-Grayman

Dreaming of the River, by Pauline Steinhorn

The series **Jewish Children in the Holocaust** consists of the following autobiographies of Jewish children
hidden during WWII in the Netherlands:

Searching for Home. The Impact of WWII on a Hidden Child,
by Joseph Gosler

Sounds from Silence. Reflections of a Child Holocaust Survivor, Psychiatrist and Teacher, by Robert Krell

Sabine's Odyssey. A Hidden Child and her Dutch Rescuers,
by Agnes Schipper

The Journey of a Hidden Child,
by Harry Pila and Robin Black

The series **New Jewish Fiction** consists of the following novels, written by Jewish authors. All novels are set in the time during or after the Holocaust.

The Corset Maker. A Novel, by Annette Libeskind Berkovits

Escaping the Whale. The Holocaust is over. But is it ever over for the next generation? by Ruth Rotkowitz

When the Music Stopped. Willy Rosen's Holocaust, by Casey Hayes

Hands of Gold. One Man's Quest to Find the Silver Lining in Misfortune, by Roni Robbins

The Girl Who Counted Numbers. A Novel, by Roslyn Bernstein

There was a garden in Nuremberg. A Novel, by Navina Michal Clemerson

The Butterfly and the Axe, by Omer Bartov

To Live Another Day. A Novel, by Elizabeth Rosenberg

The Right to Happiness. After all they went through. Stories, by Helen Schary Motro

Five Amber Beads, by Richard Aronowitz

To Love Another Day. A Novel, by Elizabeth Rosenberg

Cursing the Darkness. A Novel about Loss and Recovery, by Joanna Rosenthall

The series **Holocaust Heritage** consists of the following memoirs by 2G:

The Cello Still Sings. A Generational Story of the Holocaust and of the Transformative Power of Music, by Janet Horvath

The Fire and the Bonfire. A Journey into Memory, by Ardyn Halter

The Silk Factory: Finding Threads of My Family's True Holocaust Story, by Michael Hickins

Winter Light. The Memoir of a Child of Holocaust Survivors, by Grace Feuerverger

Out from the Shadows. Growing up with Holocaust Survivor Parents, by Willie Handler

Hidden in Plain Sight. A Family Memoir and the Untold Story of the Holocaust in Serbia, by Julie Brill

The Unspeakable. Breaking my family's silence surrounding the Holocaust, by Nicola Hanefeld

Eighteen for Life. Surviving the Holocaust, by Helen Schamroth

Four Survivor Grandparents. Run. Rely. Rebuild, by Jonathan Schloss

Austrian Again. Reclaiming a Lost Legacy, by Anne Hand

The series **Holocaust Books for Young Adults** consists of the following novels, based on true stories:

The Boy behind the Door. How Salomon Kool Escaped the Nazis. Inspired by a True Story, by David Tabatsky

Running for Shelter. A True Story, by Suzette Sheft

The Precious Few. An Inspirational Saga of Courage based on True Stories, by David Twain with Art Twain

Dark Shadows Hover, by Jordan Steven Sher

The Sun will Shine Again, by Cynthia Goldstein Monsour

The Memory Place, by Monica van Rijn

The series **WWII Historical Fiction** consists of the following novels, some of which are based on true stories:

Mendelevski's Box. A Heartwarming and Heartbreaking Jewish Survivor's Story, by Roger Swindells

A Quiet Genocide. The Untold Holocaust of Disabled Children in WWII Germany, by Glenn Bryant

The Knife-Edge Path, by Patrick T. Leahy

Brave Face. The Inspiring WWII Memoir of a Dutch/German Child, by I. Caroline Crocker and Meta A. Evenbly

When We Had Wings. The Gripping Story of an Orphan in Janusz Korczak's Orphanage. A Historical Novel, by Tami Shem-Tov

Jacob's Courage. Romance and Survival amidst the Horrors of War, by Charles S. Weinblatt

A Semblance of Justice. Based on true Holocaust experiences, by Wolf Holles

Under the Pink Triangle. Where forbidden love meets unspeakable evil, by Katie Moore

Amsterdam Publishers Newsletter

Subscribe to our Newsletter by selecting the menu at the top (right) of
amsterdampublishers.com

www.ingramcontent.com/pod-product-compliance
Lightning Source LLC
LaVergne TN
LVHW091546070526
838199LV00024B/563/J